Research on Management Technology of Sea Area Reclamation

Research on Management Technology of Sea Area Reclamation

Anning Suo

South China Sea Institute of Oceanology, Chinese Academy of Sciences, China

Yonghai Yu

National Marine Environment Monitoring Center, China

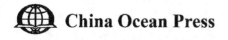 China Ocean Press

 World Scientific

Published by

World Scientific Publishing Co. Pte. Ltd.

5 Toh Tuck Link, Singapore 596224

USA office: 27 Warren Street, Suite 401-402, Hackensack, NJ 07601

UK office: 57 Shelton Street, Covent Garden, London WC2H 9HE

Library of Congress Cataloging-in-Publication Data
Names: Suo, Anning, author. | Yu, Yonghai, author.
Title: Research on management technology of sea area reclamation / Anning Suo,
　　South China Sea Institute of Oceanology, Chinese Academy of Sciences, China;
　　Yonghai Yu, National Marine Environment Monitoring Center, China.
Other titles: Wei tian hai guan li ji shu yan jiu. English
Description: Singapore ; Hackensack, NJ : World Scientific, [2022] |
　　Includes bibliographical references and index.
Identifiers: LCCN 2021053061 | ISBN 9789811246388 (hardcover) |
　　ISBN 9789811246395 (ebook for institutions) | ISBN 9789811246401 (ebook for individuals)
Subjects: LCSH: Reclamation of land--China. | Seashore--China. |
　　Environmental management--China.
Classification: LCC S605 .S76 2022 | DDC 627/.5--dc23/eng/20211208
LC record available at https://lccn.loc.gov/2021053061

British Library Cataloguing-in-Publication Data
A catalogue record for this book is available from the British Library.

围填海管理技术研究
Originally published in Chinese by China Ocean Press Ltd.
Copyright © China Ocean Press Ltd., 2017

For any available supplementary material, please visit
https://www.worldscientific.com/worldscibooks/10.1142/12530#t=suppl

Desk Editors: Jayanthi Muthuswamy/Steven Patt

Typeset by Stallion Press
Email: enquiries@stallionpress.com

Printed in Singapore

Preface

Coastal reclamation is one of the major activities in coastal development and exploitation in China. State leaders, researchers, and news media, among others, are concerned about the management of coastal reclamation. In recent years, China's State Oceanic Administration (SOA) has led continuous research on management techniques for coastal reclamation as part of its efforts to promote a standardized management approach. The National Marine Environmental Monitoring Center (NMEMC) and the SOA's Key Laboratory of Sea-Area Management Technology are two prominent organizations responsible for technological research and operational support for the management of sea areas in China. Their work in recent years has included the development of a comprehensive set of techniques, methods, and tools for the following tasks: (1) investigating the drivers behind large-scale coastal reclamation in China and forecasting demands for coastal reclamation, (2) demonstrating and evaluating the suitability of coastal reclamation projects, (3) Plan management for coastal reclamation, (4) making regional sea-use planning for construction projects, (5) dynamic monitoring of coastal reclamation activities, (6) controlling the area of coastal reclamation and promoting the intensive use of the reclaimed land, (7) accepting coastal reclamation projects upon completion, and (8) assessing projects after completion.

This book summarizes the technological research on coastal reclamation by the NMEMC in 10 chapters, covering: (1) current management practices at the national and global level, (2) drivers behind China's large-scale coastal reclamation activities, (3) guidelines for designing regional sea-use plans for construction projects, (4) Plan management for coastal

v

reclamation, (5) control of the total area of coastal reclamation activities, (6) promotion of the intensive use of the reclaimed land, (7) dynamic monitoring and evaluation of coastal reclamation activities, (8) acceptance of projects upon completion, and (9) post assessment of coastal reclamation projects. We expect that this book can be of use to regulators, assessors, owners, and other stakeholders in understanding the management of coastal reclamation in China. Teachers and students who are interested in the study and teaching of coastal reclamation management might also use it as a comprehensive, objective, and systematic technical textbook.

This book is a joint work of the NMEMC and related technical professionals. Specifically, the chapters and their contributors are as follows: *Chapter 1*: Anning Suo, Yonghai Yu, and Youliang Xu; *Chapter 2*: Ke Cao, Jie Huang, and Aiqing Han; *Chapter 3*: Anning Suo, Binyong Li, and Quanming Wang; *Chapter 4*: Yonghai Yu and AnningSuo; *Chapter 5*: Anning Suo, Jie Huang, and Yonghai Yu; *Chapter 6*: Hongwei Ma, Binyong Li, and Yueyin Cai; *Chapter 7*: Houjun Wang and Daowei Yuan; *Chapter 8*: Peng Wang, Qinbang Sun, and Kai Jia; *Chapter 9*: Anning Suo, Daowei Yuan, and Jishun Yan; *Chapter 10*: Aiqing Han and Anning Suo. The draft version of this book has been edited and finalized by Anning Suo and Yonghai Yu. Even though the authors have strived to avoid any deficiencies in this book, the readers' comments and suggestions would be greatly appreciated.

The readers interested in the theories and technical studies of coastal reclamation management can also visit the Key Laboratory of Sea-Area Management Technology under the SOA for a direct discussion and interaction.

About the Authors

**Anning Suo** is now working in the South China Sea Institute of Oceanology, Chinese Academy of Sciences (CAS), and his research interests lie in marine environmental monitoring and assessment, seascape ecology, and sea ranch ecosystem ecology as a professor. He was chosen as an expert in the state-level expert group of sea-area use and sea-area use management. He has published more than 110 papers (60 papers were as the first author). In addition, he is the first author of seven monographs including *Remote Sensing Monitoring and Assessment of Coastal Development, Remote Sensing Monitoring and Assessment of Sea Uses,* and *Management Technology of Sea Area Reclamation.* As a holder of five patent rights and a reviewer of the National Natural Science Foundation of China, he has been awarded first prize in marine engineering technology once, second prize in marine engineering technology twice, second prize in marine science and technology once, and Marine Outstanding Book Award once. He was chosen as hundred-level talent of the "hundred million" project in Liaoning Province, China,in 2015.

Yonghai Yu is now working in the National Marine Environment Monitoring Center, China. He is dean of the Academy of Marine Comprehensive treatment of the National Marine Environment Monitoring Center and the director of the Key Laboratory of sea-area management technology of the State Oceanic Administration. He is also a member of the Jiu San Society, Dalian Municipal Committee. For a long time, he has been mainly engaged in the research of sea-area management policy systems, technical methods, and the renovation and restoration of the marine ecological environment. He has academically been involved in the following: a member of the National Marine Standardization Technical Committee, an expert of the China Pacific Society, a reviewer expert of sea area utilization demonstration, a reviewer expert of the environmental impact statement of marine engineering construction project, an expert of the LiaoNing high-level science and technology expert database in 2010, a member of Dalian Leading talent training plan in 2015, and a member of the editorial board and a director of journals such as *Geography and Geo-Information Science*, *Journal of Geomatics*, and *Marine Environmental Science*. His scientific research projects have been awarded the first and second prizes by the Marine Engineering Science and Technology of China Association of Oceanic Engineering and the second prize of the Marine Science and Technology award of the State Oceanic Administration.

Contents

Introduction

Sea-area reclamation is one of the main activities in marine development and utilization in China; it is also a major focus point that has been concerned in the integrated management of the State Oceanic Administration of China since the 21st century. For more than 10 years, Anning Suo and Yonghai Yu have been engaged in research of sea-area reclamation management technology and have recommended the research results to the administrative department. This book is a phased summary of the research on sea-area reclamation management technology in the past 10 years in China, including the contents of the socio-economic driving force mechanism, planning management, total quantity control, dynamic monitoring, intensive utilization, final checkup for acceptance of reclamation, and post assessment of reclamation. Among these technologies, planning management, dynamic monitoring, and post assessment techniques for sea-area reclamation are widely used in the practice of reclamation management in China and have been unanimously recognized by the management department. Above all, sea-area reclamation management technologies form a technical system for sea-area reclamation management with Chinese characteristics. This book provides a window for reviewing and understanding sea-area reclamation management in China for domestic and foreign reclamation managers, reclamation researchers and technicians, owners of reclamation projects, and related communities who want to understand China's reclamation management. This book was selected to be a part of the publishing program of the "13th Five-Year Plan" in

China; it was also a part of the Marine Ecological Civilization series books. It won the excellent book award of the China Oceanographic Society in 2018. It is a relatively comprehensive, objective, and systematic textbook of reclamation management technology for teachers and students interested in marine management.

Chapter 1

Overview of Management Measures for Coastal Reclamation

1.1 Overview of Coastal Reclamation in China

Sea enclosure involves the flanking of sea areas for coastal development using embankments or similar structures. The enclosed areas are utilized for aquaculture as salt evaporation ponds or as water reservoirs. Land reclamation also involves the building of embankments to enclose sea areas, but its purpose is to provide new land. Coastal reclamation is defined as encompassing both sea enclosure and land reclamation (Yonghai Yu and Suo Anning, 2013a); in this book, however, coastal reclamation refers mostly to land reclamation. China has a long history of coastal reclamation. The basic concept can be traced back to a folk tale, according to which "a bird named Jingwei (literally, 'Spirit Guardian') carried pebbles and twigs from the mountains in the west and dropped them into the sea in the east because it was determined to fill up the sea." According to historical records, an industry was developed over 2,000 years ago during the Western Han Dynasty (206 BC–220 AD) in the Haiyan county on the northern banks of the Hangzhou Bay for boiling brine to produce salt in salt farms on sea tidal flats. Yiying Lu had written in *Records of Shenshiqiao* (1186, or the thirteenth year of Chunxi, the Southern Song Dynasty) that "this residential area (in the Song Dynasty) was sea in the Qin Dynasty, a tidal flat in the Han Dynasty, and a salt-producing site in the Tang Dynasty." His work records the historical process of enclosing the sea's tidal flats for cultivation (Xu Chengxiang and Yongqiang Yu, 2003). For the "three northern plains" of the southern bank of the Hang zhou

1

Bay—Yuyao, Cixi, and the Zhenhai counties—the earliest available record of embankment building dates back to 1047 (the seventh year of Qingli in the Northern Song Dynasty). By 1341 (the first year of Zhizheng in the Yuan Dynasty), an ancient embankment of 70 km had been formed. It connected Shangyu at its west end and Yangpu, in Cixi, at the east end. This ancient embankment separated the sea along its northern bank from the land between its southern bank and the mountains. It was extended to Longtouchang in the east during the Hongzhi period of the Ming Dynasty. With the expansion of the tidal flats, the ancient embankment was used for building more embankments toward the coastline. By 2001, 10 embankments had been built, and currently, there are up to 11 embankments in some locations. The embankments have migrated outward by about 16 km.

For the period from 1949 to the present, coastal reclamation in China can be divided into four stages. The first stage was characterized by the establishment of many salt farms along the coastline immediately after the founding of the People's Republic of China. The salt farms were set up in all of the 11 coastal provinces (as well as in municipalities directly under the central government and the autonomous regions). They could be found along the coastline from the Liaodong Peninsula to the Hainan Island. The Changlu salt area, which was established and expanded during this stage, is now the largest salt area in China. The Hainan Yingge sea salt farm, the biggest in Southern China, was established and put into operation in 1958. The salt farms established during this stage were mostly parallel to the coastline. The most obvious environmental impact was sediment accretion on the tidal flats.

The second stage ranged from the middle of the 1960s to the 1970s and was marked by a large-scale reclamation for more agricultural land. For example, in the Shantou Port, 22 lots were reclaimed between 1949 and 1978, covering a total area of 5,800 hm^2. In the Fujian Province, the reclaimed agricultural land covered about 75,000 hm^2, and in Shanghai, an area of 33,300 hm^2 was reclaimed for agricultural land. In this stage, the reclaimed lands were also mostly parallel to the coastline. However, they were no longer restricted to the high tidal flats, being located in the middle and low flats. Large areas of inshore tidal flats disappeared during this stage.

The third stage, ranging from the late1980s to the early 1990s, represented a period of reclamation for aquaculture. Most reclamation activities took place on low tidal flats and inshore waters. Extensive aquaculture led to substantial eutrophication.

The fourth stage, the 21st century, has been a period of reclamation for land. From Liaoning to Guangxi, the coastal provinces and cities in

China have implemented coastal reclamation works of various areas to build industrial areas, coastal tourism areas, new towns, and large infrastructures. These works aim to provide more space for production and residence in coastal areas. The reclamation at this stage has mostly been driven by the demand for resolving the issue of limited land resources because the lack of land resources seriously hinders economic and social development in coastal areas. Hence, coastal reclamation has become a vital tool for expanding the space for production and living (Yonghai Yu and Suo Anning, 2013b).

Since the turn of the 21st century, the scale of coastal reclamation in China has increased continuously as a result of growing coastal development activities. According to the SOA's *National Sea-Area Use Management Bulletin*, by the end of 2015, the total land area from coastal reclamation with registered use rights had reached 154,900 hm² (China started to register sea-area use rights in 1993). In 2006–2010 (China's 11th Five-Year Plan period), the area increased at the highest rate since the founding of the People's Republic of China, reaching a peak of 17,900 hm² in 2009. Since then, the implementation of a plan-management system for coastal reclamation activities has put a brake on the rapid growth. From 2011 through 2015 (the 12th Five-Year Plan period), the total area added nationwide was 56,600 hm², which was 10,600 hm² less than that during the 11th Five-Year Plan. The average annual area of the land that has been reclaimed and registered was 11,300 hm². The nationwide trend in the registered and reclaimed area for the period 2005–2015 is shown in Figure 1.1.

In terms of regional distribution, coastal reclamation activities in the last 10 years in China have mainly been concentrated in the Liaodong Bay, Bohai Bay, and Laizhou Bay, along the coast of the Bohai Sea; the Haizhou Bay and the extensive tidal flats in the northern Jiangsu Province, along the coast of the Yellow Sea; the Hangzhou Bay, Oujiang Estuary, and some bays in the Fujian Province, along the coast of the East China Sea; the Pearl River Estuary, Beibu Bay, and Dapeng Bay, along the coast of the South China Sea; and the sea area to the northwest of the Hainan Province in the South China Sea. During 2006–2010, the Zhejiang Province added an area of 11,137.12 hm² from coastal reclamation, accounting for 16.57% of the national total area in the same period. It was followed by the Jiangsu Province (10,503.79 hm², which includes 2,037.00 hm² for agriculture), Fujian Province (9,440.54 hm², which includes 1,594.12 hm² for agriculture), Liaoning province (9,406.23 hm²), and Tianjin (8,494.20 hm²), accounting for 15.63%, 14.05%, 14.00%, and 12.64% of the national total, respectively.

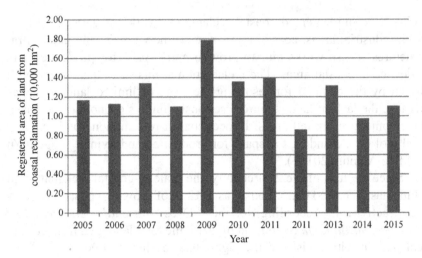

Figure 1.1 The trend in registered reclaimed area nationwide for 2005–2015.

In contrast, in Guangdong, Hainan, Guangxi, and Shanghai, the reclaimed areas were below 3,500 hm² in the past five years.

As to the uses of the reclaimed land, the focus has shifted from building ports to the development of the coastal economic zones and industrial areas (Zhiqiang Gao *et al.*, 2014). For instance, in order to accommodate the Shougang steel plants, which were to be relocated, the plan for the Caofeidian Industrial Park involved the reclamation of a land area of 31,000 hm², which had almost been achieved by 2015. To expand the urban development space, the Tianjin Binhai New Area has planned to reclaim 25,000 hm² from the sea, and the target has largely been achieved. Of the 11,397 hm² area to be reclaimed, according to the plan for the Changxing Island Lingang Industrial Park in Liaoning, 3,391 hm² has thus far been reclaimed. Moreover, in provinces such as Jiangsu and Zhejiang, large areas of land have been reclaimed to develop modern agriculture and compensate for lost arable land.

1.2 China's Practices of Coastal Reclamation Management

China has adopted a rigorous approach to the management of coastal reclamation. For example, the 2002 Law of the People's Republic of China on the Administration of the Use of Sea Areas specified that "The State strictly controls sea-use activities such as sea enclosure and land reclamation that change the natural properties of a sea area." National Marine Functional Zoning (2011–2020) requires that "reclamation should be reasonable and moderate while coastal nature reserve zones should be protected with strict measures" and that "reclamation activities in the bay areas should be rigorously controlled." In 2003, Premier Jiabao Wen gave the following declaration at the 28th Executive Meeting of the State Council: "We must take a tough stance in regulating coastal development and exploitation, especially land reclamation and sea-sand mining." In August 2013, during a group study session of the Political Bureau of the Communist Party of China's Central Committee, President Jinping Xi called for a strict control of the coastal reclamation activities. Over the years, a series of policies and systems for the complete life-cycle management of the coastal reclamation activities developed and implemented by the SOA has had a positive effect on coastal reclamation management in China. Figure 1.2 summarizes the measures adopted by the relevant authorities for each stage in the complete lifecycle of the coastal reclamation activities (Xinchun Pan, 2014).

In general, the measures cover six dimensions—holistic zoning, planning guidance, adjustment of plans, scientific demonstration, strict examination and approval, and enhanced supervision—to optimize the spatial distribution of sea-use projects, control the area of these projects, change sea-use methods, and promote intensive sea-use.

1.2.1 *China Has Developed a Legal Framework for Strengthening the Management and Control of Coastal Reclamation*

The Law of the People's Republic of China on the Administration of the Use of Sea Areas stipulates that projects that reclaim more than 50 hm² of land area from the sea and enclose a sea area of more than 100 hm² must be submitted to the State Council for examination and approval. The Island Protection Law of the People's Republic of China specifies that "activities such as land reclamation and sea enclosure that change the coastline of inhabited islands should be strictly restricted; the same applies to projects that involve land reclamation works for connecting adjacent islands." Article 7 of the People's Republic of China's Regulations on Prevention and Control of Pollution and Damages to the Marine

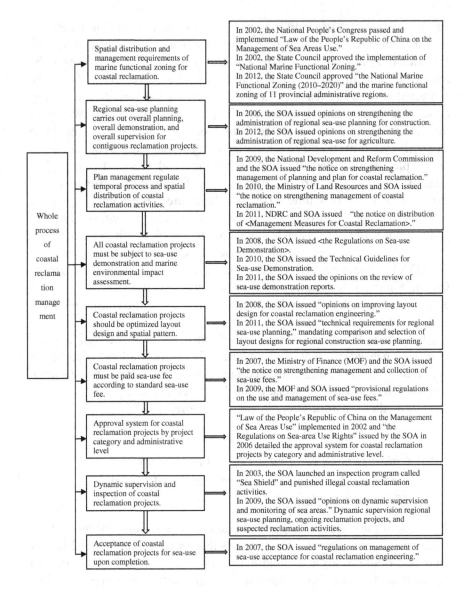

Figure 1.2 National reclamation management process based on coastal reclamation full activities.

Environment by Coastal Engineering Construction Projects specifies that "Land reclamation projects are not allowed in areas of natural bays with potential for shipping purposes; important seedling bases, breeding grounds, and related water surfaces; natural spawning grounds, breeding grounds, and feeding grounds in tidal flats; and important migration routes for fish, shrimp, crabs, shellfish, or algae. Land reclamation is not permitted in non-alluvial coastal areas of bays or other semi-closed waters."

1.2.2 *Holistic Coordination and Restriction of Spatial Distribution by Marine Functional Zoning*

In 2012, the State Council approved the implementation of National Marine Functional Zoning (2011–2020) and the subsequent marine functional zoning of 11 provinces (or autonomous regions and municipalities directly under the central government). This zoning provides a critical basis for the management of sea use and the protection of the marine environment at both the national and regional levels. Marine functional zoning precisely demarcates the sea areas for industrial and urban construction, ports and shipping, and tourism and leisure. It coordinates the area and spatial distribution of coastal reclamation projects holistically at the national level. In other words, all the construction projects must comply with the zoning requirements and be located in the relevant basic functional zones. Coastal reclamation activities are strictly prohibited in prominent ecological protection areas, fishermen's usual breeding areas, coastal landscapes, and tourist areas. Projects that do not conform to the marine functional zoning will be rejected.

1.2.3 *Adjustment to the Temporal Distribution of Coastal Reclamation Projects through Annual Plan Management*

Since 2010, China has adopted an annual Plan-management approach for coastal reclamation projects. Each provincial administrative region is required to maintain records on annual Plan indicators to ensure that the area of the coastal reclamation activities is within limits determined by the indicators. The national coastal reclamation Plan is included in the annual plan for national economic and social development according to set procedures. The Plan is divided into projects for construction and agriculture, and the two categories must be used separately. For coastal reclamation projects in the regional reclamation plan, the Plan is amortized annually on the basis of the approval of the projects.

1.2.4 *Regional Sea-Use Planning to Limit the Concentration of Coastal Reclamation Projects*

For clusters of coastal reclamation projects for urban or rural development, a holistic planning report for regional sea-use must be compiled to prevent the cumulative impact of multiple coastal reclamation projects on the ecological environment. The regional sea-use plan should ensure a holistic planning of projects within the region and should promote a reasonable layout, thereby promoting a sound development and effective use of sea resources. The regional sea-use plans include plans for construction and agriculture.

1.2.5 *Strengthening the Management of the Layout Design of Coastal Reclamation*

In 2008, the SOA issued Opinions on Improving Layout Design for Coastal Reclamation Works. This document required that the layout design should follow the principles of protecting natural shorelines, effectively increasing artificial shorelines, and improving the effectiveness of the coastal landscape. As far as possible, the layout designs for coastal reclamation should adopt the use of multiple blocks in combination, artificial islands and multi-jetties.

1.2.6 *Analysis of the Suitability of Coastal Reclamation Projects by Demonstration and Evaluation*

The SOA requires that all the coastal reclamation projects should be subjected to sea-use demonstration and a marine environmental impact assessment, covering the suitability of the project's location, area, use, layout, and environmental impact. To ensure a reasonable sea-use, projects involving inappropriate locations, excessive area, waste of shoreline resources, or severe damage to the environment should be rejected.

1.2.7 *Strengthening Coastal Reclamation Management through the Principle of User Pays and Compensates*

China adopts the principle of user pays for coastal reclamation. Organizations and individuals are required to pay royalty fees for the use of sea areas, and the royalty fees are differentiated according to the use.

The highest rate is RMB 1.8 million Yuan/hm^2, and the fees are collected in a lump sum. The users should also compensate for any economic losses suffered by the stakeholders in surrounding areas.

1.2.8 *Rigorous Examination and Approval of Coastal Reclamation Projects*

All coastal reclamation projects must be subject to the examination and approval of the State Council or provincial governments. Before submitting the project feasibility study report or project application report, the contractor of the coastal reclamation project must first apply for the use of the sea area with the national or provincial authority for marine administration in line with the law. The provincial authority for marine administration will conduct a preliminary examination based on marine functional zoning, the sea-use demonstration report, and the evaluation opinions of experts. After this examination, it should provide preliminary results. The State Council and provincial governments, while ensuring that the demands for sea-use from the key marine industries and key national energy facilities, transportation facilities, and other major infrastructure requirements are met, will firmly reject projects that are restricted or prohibited by the national industrial policies or that could have a substantial impact on the environmental resources and ecological systems according to the assessment by the experts.

1.2.9 *Dynamic Monitoring of the Construction Process of Coastal Reclamation Projects*

To ensure the orderly development of coastal resources, China established a dynamic supervision and monitoring system for the construction process of coastal reclamation projects in 2006. This system, which operates at the national, provincial, city, and county levels, could identify and report illegal coastal reclamation activities in real time. Site inspections are required to focus on coastal reclamation projects that had not been approved or that had changed their use or scope.

1.2.10 *Coastal Reclamation Projects Must Be Accepted upon Completion before Putting into Use*

A marine administrative authority must accept a coastal reclamation project upon its completion before it is put into use. The project is checked based on a range of criteria, including on-site measurement; a survey; a careful check of the location, scope, area, and layout against the requirements in the approval documentation; the implementation of the project and management measures; and the treatment of the project's stakeholders.

1.3 Management of Coastal Reclamation in Other Countries

In coastal countries with scarce land resources, coastal reclamation is an important route for expanding the land area for development. These countries are mainly found in four regions: East and Southeast Asia (China, Japan, South Korea, and Singapore), the Persian Gulf (Dubai, Qatar, etc.); Europe (Netherlands, Greece, Germany, UK, France, etc.); and the American regions (the United States, Mexico, etc.). These countries have adopted different measures for managing coastal reclamation based on their resources and the projects' environmental impact.

1.3.1 *Management of Coastal Reclamation in Japan*

Japan had started coastal reclamation activities at an extremely early stage, but in the initial stage before 1945, these activities mainly provided land for agricultural and industrial development. After the Second World War, Japan's industries recovered and developed rapidly, and coastal reclamation activities expanded accordingly. By 1978, 73,700 hm^2 of land had been reclaimed, most of which was used for ports and harbor industries. From 1979 to 1986, Japan had initiated a structural adjustment of the reclamation activities. The land reclaimed at this stage was mostly used in the tertiary sector. With more importance being attached to environmental benefits, the area and speed of coastal reclamation activities were significantly reduced. In the 1990s, Japan's economic growth slowed. The area of land reclaimed dropped continuously with the reduced demand for land and increased public concerns about the impact of coastal reclamation on the ecological environment. The total area of land reclaimed since then has stabilized at a level of 500 hm^2 per year.

In 1921, to manage coastal reclamation activities, the Japanese government promulgated the Public Water Reclamation Law, regulating such issues as the licensing of coastal reclamation, collection of royalty fees, and the ownership of the reclaimed land. In 1973, the government issued the Revision to the Public Water Reclamation Law, strengthening requirements on the use of the reclaimed land and reviewing the environmental impact. The key to coastal reclamation management in Japan is the reclamation permit. To obtain a reclamation permit, land reclamation applicants have to apply to a prefectural governor after coordination with stakeholders and an assessment of the environmental impact. The prefectural governor must first examine the application and then publish the details for public comments, including contributions from local villages, local authorities, maritime safety agencies, environmental protection bureaus, local public organizations, and other relevant agencies. After evaluating the comments, the governor considers the treatment of the stakeholders, the scope of the project, the area of reclamation, the guarantee of public spaces, the royalty fees, the construction process, and the project's utility. An application is then filed with the Ministry of Land, Infrastructure, Transport, and Tourism (MLIT) for approval of the license. The MLIT will review the application and present its opinions to the governor, who will issue the license to the applicant on the basis of these opinions. The Japanese government maintains a neutral position of "providing no incentives and imposing no restrictions" in the management of coastal reclamation. Market demands drive the extent of coastal reclamation through a market mechanism.

Instead, Japan focuses on the holistic planning of the coastal reclamation projects on three levels. First, it has an overall plan for the development of the coastal areas, which mainly involves the establishment and functional positioning of several key development areas. Second, for these key areas, such as larger bays with industrial belts, the overall spatial planning has been developed, including plans for interconnected urban areas, the development of bays, and marine functional planning. At this level, the coastal line of a region is divided into several basic functional sections with clearly defined functional positioning of specific sections and the adjacent waters. Under the guidance provided by the plan, coastal reclamation projects are located in a specific functional section according to the use. The third level involves the layout and forms a design of the coastal reclamation projects within each basic functional section. According to the guidance provided at this level, most of the projects are in the form of artificial islands extending outward to the sea. Only a few are parallel to the coastline. It is also common for a project to be divided by waterways; projects with a large area of continuous land are rare. Moreover, the shoreline of the reclaimed land is generally in the form of curves instead of in a straight line (Li Sun, 2009).

1.3.2 *Management of Coastal Reclamation in the Netherlands*

The Netherlands is located in northern Europe, on the coast of the Atlantic Ocean's North Sea. It is in the lower estuaries of the Meuse, Rhine, and Scheldt rivers and is a part of the coastal plain of Western Europe. Since the 13th century, the land of the Netherlands has been eroded by the North Sea by an area of more than 5,600 km^2. For prevention and protection against floods and expansion of its inhabited land, the Netherlands has carried out large-scale land reclamation activities in the past 800 years, covering an area of 5,200 km^2. This long history of reclamation can be divided into four stages: The first stage, from the 13th to 16th centuries, was characterized by slow development. Major coastal reclamation activities involved the installation of wave barriers made by wooden piles and branches in shallow sea areas from natural sedimentation. The barriers promoted the formation of land by facilitating sedimentation. The second stage, from the 17th to 19th centuries, saw a rapid growth in coastal reclamation activities. This stage also coincided with the period in which the Netherlands became more powerful with advances in technology. Alongside improved windmills, which were capable of draining water from enclosed areas more efficiently, an even greater investment in coastal reclamation rapidly drove the extent of the reclaimed land up to about 3,000 km^2. The third stage, during the 20th century, was the heyday of coastal reclamation. In this stage, diesel engines and electric power were used instead of steam power to build dikes and drainage facilities, due to which an area of 1,650 km^2 of reclaimed land was added. In the fourth stage, during the 21st century, the process was reversed, with about 100 km^2 of land being returned to the sea to harmonize the relationship between humans and nature.

A comprehensive planning and assessment system support the management of coastal reclamation in the Netherlands. The country has extensive plans at the national level for wetlands, seashore protection, marine protection zones, water resource recycling, and delta development. In addition, it has an integrated technological system for assessing reclaimed areas. For post assessment of coastal reclamation projects, the technologies include mathematical and physical modeling technologies on seashore stability, wave flows, navigation under wave flows, seabed topography, and safe passage of flood flows, as well as mathematical modeling for the ecological environment of wave tidal currents and tidal gradient change. This assessment covers the effects of coastal reclamation on sea-level changes, future river flows, land subsidence, and the gradient of the tidal prism. The country has also developed a system of quantitative assessment technologies related to coastal reclamation. They include technologies for assessing biological resources, the natural habitat ecosystem, navigation capacity, seashore stability, seabed erosion, marine environmental quality, effects of coastal reclamation on the passage of flood flows and tidal prism, and the effects on coastal passages (Rongjun Li, 2006). In the Netherlands, the government conducts comprehensive cost-benefit analyses of the stages of construction and operation of coastal reclamation and seashore projects, such as evaluations of the economic costs and benefits of the projects, analyses of the impact on local and external resources and the environment, and analyses of the direct and indirect impacts of the construction process. In addition, the Netherlands has an established system for engaging the public in the government's decision-making and parliament's deliberative processes (Qixiang He *et al.*, 2002).

1.3.3 *Management of Coastal Reclamation in South Korea*

South Korea's coastal reclamation activities started in the early 20th century, mainly to increase arable land and address the shortage of agricultural land. Between 1910 and 1945, a total of 408.80 km^2 of land was reclaimed, mostly scattered across small, high tidal flats in bay areas. Between 1950 and 1990, South Korea's coastal reclamation activities increased substantially, with more than 1,000 km^2 of land reclaimed. The land was mostly used for water conservancy projects, industrial construction, and transportation, as well as other purposes. After 1990, as the public became increasingly concerned about the environmental impact of coastal reclamation activities, the government began to adopt a prudent reclamation policy, under which annual reclamation activities declined considerably.

Critical measures for coastal reclamation management in South Korea include the establishment of a sound legal framework, the control of the total area of the coastal reclamation activities, extensive public participation, and prudent reclamation management policies. South Korea promulgated its Law on the Management of Public Water in 1961 and the Law on the Reclamation of Public Water in 1962. Essential planning for public water reclamation based on the laws is intended to be re-developed every 10 years and reviewed every 5 years. Revisions to the essential planning can be made as necessary at any time. Further essential planning has imposed strict measures to limit large-scale reclamation activities, such as reclamation for arable land and urban land, expansion of new urban areas on the reclaimed land, and construction of industrial zones. The measures curbed the reclamation activities on the tidal flats to the greatest extent. Even for small-scale reclamation projects, the management measures are stringent. Projects can only be located in sea areas and public utility areas that are damaged beyond restoration or in the areas with minimal environmental losses. Moreover, these projects must be in line with the comprehensive management planning for seashore belts and must adopt construction methods that are environmentally friendly. The shift of the focus in coastal reclamation from expanding the land area to caring for the marine environment and ecological systems marked a fundamental change in the basic policy framework. As the government adjusted its stance in response to public concerns about coastal reclamation, its policies have become so prudent that only coastal reclamation projects approved by the public have a chance of being implemented. In summary, the laws, planning, expert assessments, and public participation form the basis of a sound system for the approval of applications by the South Korean government for sea use through coastal reclamation.

1.3.4 *Management of Coastal Reclamation in the Persian Gulf*

Qatar and the United Arab Emirates are among the major countries engaged in coastal reclamation along the Persian Gulf coast. Qatar's reclamation activities started at a later stage but developed rapidly with intensive investment. Its unique reclamation projects include the Pearl-Qatar, Lusail, and Museum of Islamic Art coastal reclamation projects. The distinctive features of these coastal reclamation activities include the following:

(1) *Intensive investment and lavish design*: Qatar has been obsessed with the construction of landmark buildings and a beautiful coastline landscape. For example, the Museum of Islamic Art was connected to an

artificial island with a jetty that allowed the passage of water. The island was surrounded by vertical structures along with the absence of bare, unaesthetic seashores.

(2) *Care for the water environment*: The reclaimed land was generally crisscrossed by watercourses to ensure the maximum ecological function of the reclaimed areas.

(3) *Adoption of a unique method for reclaiming land through inland excavation*: The main purpose of the reclamation activities in Qatar has been to create a beautiful coastal environment. To save materials and reduce transportation costs, the materials have been excavated from inland locations for the renovation, restoration, and development of the seashore.

Dubai is the second largest of the seven emirates that make up the United Arab Emirates. The Emirate of Dubai has proposed a grand plan to construct artificial islands on the sea to promote commercial activities and the development of leisure tourism. The plan includes the Palm Jumeirah, Jebal Ali, Deira Island, the World Islands, and Dubai Maritime City. The reclamation activities for the Palm Islands and the World Islands are largely complete. Distinctive features of these coastal reclamation activities in Dubai include the following:

(1) *Overall planning*: The Dubai artificial islands project has been a large-scale reclamation activity led by the Dubai Sheikh family. The planning, design, and development have been carried out by the Nakheel Company and controlled by the Dubai Sheikh, with government departments participating as service providers.

(2) *Extension, rather than occupation, of the natural coastline*: The artificial islands in Dubai are designed to be offshore rather than as a part of the original coastline. Moreover, the design aims at extending the coastline through the artificial islands. After completion of the project, the coastline could be increased by more than 1,000 km.

(3) *Harmony of design with the natural environment*: The project has had impressive designs, such as palms and a map of the world.

(4) *Minimization of environmental impact through dispersed development*: The Palm Islands and the World Islands incorporate many novel concepts

for large-scale reclamation projects. In particular, the islands are composed of many small blocks separated from each other to minimize their impact on the environment and to increase waterfronts (Qi Yue *et al.*, 2015).

1.3.5 *Lessons That Can Be Learnt by China in Coastal Reclamation Management from Other Countries*

China can benefit from a review of coastal reclamation management practices in two respects.

(1) *The scale and speed of coastal reclamation are positively correlated with the rate of economic development*: Demand for land area drives coastal reclamation. Reviewing the history of coastal reclamation activities in major countries, we find that the demand for land determines the extent of reclamation and that the speed of reclamation is subject to the available technologies and the urgency of the demand. The extent of the demand, the available technologies, and the urgency of the demands, in turn, reflect directly or indirectly on the rate of economic growth. In each specific period, coastal reclamation became the most effective way to expand space for development in countries experiencing a rapid economic development but having limited land space and a level of productivity that could not be improved in the short term. Thus, in countries experiencing rapid economic growth and population expansion, coastal reclamation activities were extensive and fast, whereas when economic growth and population expansion were slowing, the extent and speed of reclamation also decreased.

(2) *The uses of the reclaimed land reflect the overall levels of economic and social development*: A review of history can indicate the relationship between the level of development and the major uses of the reclaimed land. In the early stage of development, the land was mainly used for agricultural production. After the start of industrialization, most of the land was used for coastal industries and port construction. During modernization, reclamation activities focused on increasing waterfronts and serving landscape and ecological functions. Developing countries worldwide are mostly at the stage of creating land to provide development space for agriculture and industry. In developed countries, with more attention being paid to the protection of the ecological environment and landscape, the reclaimed land is mainly used to increase waterfronts.

Chapter 2

Driving Forces of Large-Scale Coastal Reclamation in China

2.1 Large-Scale Coastal Reclamation Activities Driven by Social Development

With the rapid increase in global economic integration, many petrochemical, steel, shipbuilding, and mechanical processing plants worldwide have been relocated to seashore or port areas. The trend is particularly marked in China. Along with major relocations such as the moves by the Shougang Group Co. Ltd. to Caofeidian in Hebei Province, the Angang Group Corporation, Ltd. to Bayuquan in Liaoning Province, and the Panzhihua Steel Group Co. Ltd. to Fangchenggangin Guangxi, there has also been a proliferation in emerging industries, such as marine equipment, coastal tourism, and marine biology. In coastal areas, industrial and urban development projects have competed for the space provided by coastal zones. In addition, the influx of production factors from both domestic and overseas sources has improved the infrastructure in the zones, leading to higher efficiency in regional economic activities and, thus, the expansion of new industrial and urban spaces.

In the remaining part of this section, we will discuss four ways in which the rapid industrial and urban development in China's coastal areas has driven the enormous demand for coastal reclamation.

2.1.1 *Demands for Large-Scale Coastal Reclamation Driven by the Relocation of Industrial Plants to Coastal Zones*

In recent years, China's State Council and the NDRC, in particular, have published a series of industrial revitalization plans. They envisaged a combination of advantages in terms of port, land, capital, technology, human resources, and services for the establishment of onshore and near-port industrial zones, including zones or bases for particular industries. The implementation of these plans has meant the concentration of petro-chemical, steel, energy, marine equipment manufacturing, shipping, and logistic industries in the coastal zones. China's strategy for regional development in coastal areas depends on the onshore and near-port industrial zones. They are powerful engines that accelerate regional industrialization and economic development, as well as major social forces that drive the demand for large-scale reclamation (Wei Liu, 2008; Jingmei Li *et al.*, 2012b). For example, the Caofeidian Circular Economic Zone in Hebei Province is a large-scale coastal reclamation project to accommodate the province's program for the development of coastal areas. It aims to promote the concentration of coastal industries from Beijing, Tianjin, and Hebei. At the time of writing, the total area of land reclaimed has exceeded 30,000 hm².

2.1.2 *Demands for Large-Scale Coastal Reclamation Driven by Coastal Urban Development*

According to China's coastal urban development programs, most towns will be built along the seashore to provide a pleasant living environment and well-developed land and water transportation infrastructure. The construction of coastal towns—in order to expand the urban development space, improve the urban living environment, and provide beautiful and new coastal towns—is the main driving force behind China's demand for large-scale coastal reclamation. In Tianjin, the Binhai New Area Program involved the building of an international port metropolis along the shoreline, with the selling points of an eco-friendly and comfortable living environment. Within the New Area, 5,000 hm² was designated for the business zone, 10,300 hm² for advanced manufacturing industries, 10,000 hm² for harbor logistics, 10,200 hm² for the airport industrial zone, 2,500 hm² for an onshore hi-tech industrial zone, and 8,000 hm² for an onshore chemical industrial zone. Of the 53,500 hm² total area for the program, nearly 60% was to be reclaimed land from the sea. The urban development program of

Lianyungang City proposed the idea of expanding eastward to embrace the sea with open arms. Specifically, in building its new onshore district, the city adopted a strategy of moving progressively, in three prongs, and making critical breakthroughs. The new district covers a total area of 5,800 hm^2, about 70% of which depends on coastal reclamation to provide space for development. In Wenzhou, the urban development program for the 12th Five-Year Plan involved the construction of the Oujiang River Estuary Area as the center of the city. Under the strategy of crossing the river, expansion into the sea, and concerted development along the road that surrounds the mountains, the Lingni Peninsula and Dongtou Port City functional zones will be built through coastal reclamation to expand the urban development space toward the sea. According to the program, the area of sea use will be over 10,000 hm^2. In 1990, urban construction land in coastal cities accounted for only 18.7% of the national total. In 2009, the proportion had increased to 37.3%, indicating a growth rate much higher than the national average. Of the 53 coastal prefecture-level cities in China, only Nantong, Yancheng, Putian, Shantou, Zhongshan, and Dandong have maintained growth rates of urban areas in line with the rates of urbanization. All other cities had growth rates well above their rates of urbanization (Hongbin Liu and Sun Li, 2008).

2.1.3 *Demands for Large-Scale Coastal Reclamation Driven by Rapid Development of Coastal Transportation Networks*

Since the 21st century, in a rush of port building and expansion, China has considerably increased the number, area, and handling capacity of its ports. This has resulted in five sizable port clusters in the Bohai Rim, the Yangtze River Delta, the southeast coast, the Pearl River Delta, and the southwest coast, achieved through intensive investment and the introduction of modern management methods. At present, the port shoreline is about 610 km, with more than 1,000 km in the pipeline. Given an average storage yard area of 500–800 hm^2/km, coastal port-building activities could generate a demand for coastal reclamation of 30,000 hm^2 to 500,000 hm^2. Moreover, some coastal cities have opted to expand airports or build new ones in their efforts to boost industries such as logistics and tourism. Due to the minimal land resources in coastal cities, some have decided to develop airports on the sea or to build airports on artificial islands reclaimed from the sea. Some have done so simply because others have done so. A number have adopted plans to build airports through coastal reclamation. For example, Dalian has reclaimed about 2,000 hm^2 in Jinzhou Bay to expand its civil airport.

2.1.4 *Demands for Large-Scale Coastal Reclamation Driven by the Development of Coastal Tourism*

In recent years, the strategic development programs and construction guidelines of each coastal region in China have included coastal tourism as a leading industry. The large number of planned and implemented tourism infrastructure construction projects has generated a particular demand for coastal reclamation. For example, Shandong Province proposed to build a brand of eco-tourism along the Yellow River in the Yellow River Delta area. Specifically, the province envisaged several coastal holiday tourism as well as marine sightseeing and recreational projects by relying on the "Sea-view Trestle" and the gold coast of Laizhou. A program in Jiangsu Province aimed to build Lianyungang into an internationally renowned coastal tourist city, turn the famous domestic tourist destination of Yancheng into a vital tourist city and wetland ecological tourist destination, and make Nantong into a unique "River-sea Tourism" gateway city and a famous historical and cultural city. The Yangtze River Delta region will also be turned into a system of world-class tourist destinations. Fujian Province has planned to expand the cultural boundaries of the Minnan, Hakka, and Mazu cultures on the theme of "Cross-strait Tourism" and make the region an internationally renowned tourist destination and distinctive natural and cultural center. According to another program, the Pearl River Delta area was to be a national demonstration zone for comprehensive tourism reform. It would be transformed into a famous international tourism destination and tourist hub in the Asia-Pacific region. Hainan Island has invested heavily in tropical island winter sunshine tourism, marine sports, diving, and other tourism projects in an effort to offer a large variety of tropical coastal marine tourism products. The program also involved the careful but active opening and development of Xisha tourism, as well as the orderly development of tourism on uninhabited islands. The Guangxi Zhuang Autonomous Region had ambitions to build a Pan-Beibu Gulf tourism circle based on its high-quality tourist attractions above the national 4A level. The implementation of these coastal tourism programs will drive the demand for large-scale coastal reclamation.

2.2 Large-Scale Coastal Reclamation Activities Driven by Economic Benefits

Over the past 10 years, China's land market, driven by the development of real estate, has been exceptionally prosperous. Land resources have become the core resources of regional development, and land prices have soared within a short period. Coastal reclamation is a critical way to acquire land resources in coastal areas. Generally, the cost of land from coastal reclamation in China is relatively low. It ranges from 2.1 million Yuan to 4.5 million Yuan per hectare. With suitable natural conditions for coastal reclamation, such as silt and sandy coasts, the cost could be even lower. However, the land from coastal reclamation is often transferred by auction. In small and medium-area cities, the land can be transferred at a price of more than 23 million Yuan per hectare for industrial use and 7.5 million Yuan for commercial and residential use. In coastal areas with superior locations, the price per hectare might reach nearly 10 million Yuan. The high-profit margin between the high economic gains from coastal reclamation and its lower cost is arguably the direct economic force that drives large-scale coastal reclamation activities in China (Jie Huang *et al.*, 2016b).

This economic force is determined by both the economic gains and costs of coastal reclamation. The economic gains are mostly the price of the transferred land. It can be calculated by multiplying the benchmark price, the land area from coastal reclamation, the effective land-use rate, and the plot ratio. The benchmark prices of land transfer differ for industrial land and commercial and residential land. Those for industrial land are lower and mostly in the range of 3 million to 7 million Yuan per hectare. Those for commercial and residential land are higher, generally above 10 million Yuan per hectare, albeit with substantial regional differences, and are subject to dynamic adjustment by the land authorities. The costs of coastal reclamation include sea-use fees; fees for project planning, design, demonstration, and environmental impact assessment; compensation for the loss of fishery resources; compensation for relocations; construction costs; and infrastructure costs as described as follows:

(1) *The royalty for the sea area occupied by a coastal reclamation project*: The royalty is collected nationally on the basis of sea-use types and sea-area grades according to a standard schedule. There are six grades for construction land from coastal reclamation. The standard rate for the first

grade is 300,000 Yuan per hectare. The rates increase for higher grades, up to 1.8 million Yuan per hectare for the sixth grade, and the amount is collected in a lump sum.

(2) *Fees for project planning, design, demonstration, and environmental impact assessment*: These include fees for the planning and design of coastal reclamation projects, for demonstration of sea-area use, for assessing the impact on the marine environment, and for assessing the environmental impact on waterways if the projects are related to them. Generally, these fees will not exceed 10 million Yuan for a project.

(3) *Compensation for the loss of fishery resources*: Compensation for the loss of fishery resources due to the sea area used by coastal reclamation projects is generally 10,000 Yuan per hectare.

(4) *Compensation for relocations*: If the sea area to be used by coastal reclamation was previously used for aquaculture, relocation compensation should be paid as appropriate to the former users and other stakeholders. The standard rate of compensation for relocations is usually set by the two parties through consultation and can vary substantially in different regions.

(5) *The construction costs of coastal reclamation projects*: The costs include those for dikes, backfilling (hydraulic dispersing), and land leveling. They are related to the sea terrain, hydrodynamic environment, filling materials, and the distance between the construction site and the source of the materials. They also vary in different regions.

(6) *Costs of infrastructure*: The costs of the supporting infrastructure of "seven accesses and one leveling," including those for roads, water supply, power supply, cable, telephone, and network, generally do not exceed 1 million Yuan.

As an example, consider a coastal reclamation project with an area of 250 hm^2, an effective land-use rate of 85%, and a benchmark price of 350 Yuan/m^2. The economic gain from the reclaimed land is

$$E = BP \times S \times R = 350 \text{ Yuan/m}^2 \times 2{,}500{,}000 \text{ m}^2 \times 0.85$$
$$= 743{,}750{,}000 \text{ Yuan,}$$

where BP is the benchmark price of the land in Yuan/m^2, S is the area of the land in m^2, and R is the effective land-use rate.

The costs of the reclamation project include (a) the construction cost of the dike, dredging, and dispersing: 225,442,480 Yuan; (b) earthwork backfilling and leveling cost: 5,740,277 Yuan; (c) compensation for relocations: 1,472,5000 Yuan; (d) compensation for the loss of fishery resources: 13,976,000 Yuan; (e) fees for demonstration and environmental impact assessment: 1,750,000 Yuan; (f) fees for the waterways environmental impact assessment: 150,000 Yuan; (g) sea-area royalty: 187,500,000 Yuan; and (h) costs of the infrastructure: 212,500,000 Yuan. Thus, the total cost is

$$C = \sum c_i = 22,544.248 + 574.0277 + 1,472.5 + 1,397.6 + 175 + 15 + 18,750$$
$$+ 21,250 \approx 66,178 \, (000 \, \text{Yuan}).$$

The profit for the project is

$$EP = E - C = 743,750,000 - 661,780,000 = 81,970,000 \, \text{Yuan}.$$

That is, with an area of 250 hm^2, the land for industrial use could be transferred at 743,750,000 Yuan. As the standard rate of royalty for a fourth-grade sea area is 750,000 Yuan per hectare, the royalty collectible is 187,500,000 Yuan. In addition, the comprehensive coastal reclamation costs, including the construction costs, compensation for the loss of fishery resources, sea-use royalty, and fees for sea-area demonstration and environmental impact assessment, amount to 661,780,000 Yuan. After the deduction of the total cost, the economic gain is 81,970,000 Yuan or 328,000 Yuan per hectare.

In most regions, governments are owners of coastal reclamation projects. As a certain proportion of the royalty will be retained by local governments and the compensation for the loss of fishery resources is usually not paid, the profit and the profitability rate may be higher after completing the project. The huge economic benefits are the direct cause of the coastal regions' enthusiasm for large-scale reclamation (Jie Huang *et al.*, 2016a).

2.3 Large-Scale Coastal Reclamation Activities Driven by Administrative Measures

The Land Administration Law of the People's Republic of China, enacted in 1986, allows the transfer of land-use rights, laying the foundation for the market-oriented reform of the land administration system and the system of compensated use of state-owned land resources. Under these systems and regulations, local governments have adopted an intensive rather than extensive approach to land administration by preparing overall plans according to purpose. The Decision of the Central Committee of the Communist Party of China on Several Major Issues Concerning the Promotion of Rural Reform and Development, adopted at the Third Plenary Session of the 17th Central Committee of the Communist Party of China, clearly stated that "we will adhere to the strictest possible farmland protection system by allocating responsibilities at various levels, and resolutely keep the red line of 1.2 billion hectares of farmland." With the minimum area of farmland set by the central government, local governments could not depend indefinitely on farmland to provide land needed for urbanization.

In recent years, many strategic programs and guidelines for the development of coastal areas have been approved for implementation by the State Council. These programs and guidelines include the Liaoning coastal economic zone development program, the Hebei coastal area development program, the Caofeidian industry development program for the circular economy demonstration area, the Tianjin city master plan (2005–2020), the Yellow River Delta efficient, ecological, economic zone development program, the Shandong Peninsula blue economic zone development program, the Jiangsu coastal development program, the State Council's Opinions on Promoting the Construction of an International Financial Center and International Shipping Center in Shanghai for Accelerating the Development of Modern Service Industry and Advanced Manufacturing (Shanghai's "two centers"), the economic zone development program for the west of the Taiwan Strait, the Pearl River Delta reform and development program outline (2008–2020), the development program for Guangxi Beibu Gulf Economic Zone, and Several Opinions of the State Council on Promoting the Construction and Development of the Hainan International Tourism Island. For the promotion and implementation of the strategic programs and guidelines, local governments (provinces, direct-controlled municipalities, and autonomous administrative regions) in coastal areas have included a large amount of land for industrial and urban development in their Overall Land-Use Plan and Urban and Rural Development Plan for the next 10 years. Given the strict protection of farmland and the enormous demand for industrial and urban development, reliance on coastal reclamation to provide the land needed for construction and to balance it with occupied farmland has become a widespread practice among many local government units. Statistics show that all local governments have made coastal reclamation plans for part of the land needed in their overall programs. For the next 10 years, the total area of coastal reclamation for local governments in coastal areas nationwide is set at over 520,000 hm². The area for Zhejiang Province is as much as 174,700 hm², accounting for 30% of the total. In the program for Jiangsu, the area is 71,700 hm². The area for Shanghai is 76,700 hm², while that for Shandong is 42,000 hm². Large-scale coastal reclamation could provide land urgently needed for industrial use and urban development, which have a bearing on government performance in terms of attracting investment and the construction of new urban projects. However, because of the booming real estate market, the price of construction land resources has soared in recent years, and selling land has become a "cash cow" for some local governments. The large profit margins between the low cost of reclamation and the high price of adjacent land have led some local governments to become increasingly dependent on coastal reclamation.

Some local governments have mandated the preparation of excessive sea-use programs and have carried out massive coastal reclamation projects. The land from coastal reclamation can be auctioned immediately after simple preparation and can generate billions of Yuan for local governments. Even that cannot be sold immediately can be used by local governments as collateral to obtain huge loans from banks to alleviate any financial stress. The substantial economic benefits obtained through coastal reclamation are significant reasons for governments' excessively large coastal reclamation plans. For example, in one of the hottest coastal reclamation areas—the Pan-Bohai area—there were 23 formally approved programs by the end of December 2015 that involved using the sea for construction purposes. Ten of these programs will be implemented in Liaoning, four in Hebei, three in Tianjin, and six in Shandong. The programs cover a total area of 85,240.07 hm², of which 65,093.92 hm² involves coastal reclamation projects. It can be concluded that economic benefits are the main driving force behind the large-scale coastal reclamation activities in the 12th and 13th Five-Year Plan periods.

2.4 Large-Scale Coastal Reclamation Activities Driven by Government Policies

The 2002 Law of the People's Republic of China on the Administration of Sea Use established ownership management, the principle of user pays, and three basic systems for the administration of marine functional zoning. It ensured the orderly, paid, and appropriate use of China's sea areas. In 2006, China began to implement the system of regional sea-use planning for construction purposes, requiring the holistic demonstration and submission of planning compiled for the development of sea areas in clusters. In 2012, the State Council approved National Marine Functional Zoning (2011–2020) and the marine functional zoning of 11 provincial administrative regions along the coast, imposing dual limits on the use and total area of coastal reclamation. In 2012, the NDRC and SOA jointly issued the Notice on Strengthening the Plan Management in Planning Coastal Reclamation Projects and the Plan Management of Coastal Reclamation, according to which, "reclamation activities must involve Plan management, which is mandatory and should be overridden without proper authorization." Currently, China's management of coastal reclamation can be characterized as "overall planning, guiding on programs, Plan adjustment, scientific demonstration, strict approval, and enhanced supervision."

However, for several reasons, the current management of coastal reclamation in China still leaves room for large-scale reclamation.

(1) Local governments and other stakeholders restrict the preparation of marine functional zoning. The final output is mostly the result of a multi-party game, and the task of maintaining the natural attributes of the marine ecosystem is not at the top of the agenda.

(2) The Plan management is not valid. In some areas, local governments manipulate the indicators or apply for excessive Plans so that the total Plan is decided by their development needs.

(3) The regional sea-use planning for construction purposes and the Plan management for coastal reclamation do not function seamlessly. The regional sea-use planning for construction purposes generally has a horizon of 5–10 years, while Plan management applies to the sea-use area in a specified year. The Plan might not be applied for a specific year's regional sea-use planning application, which is a way of requesting a larger plan for subsequent years.

(4) The sea-area management framework still lacks effective standards for reviewing regional planning and individual coastal reclamation projects in

order to control the area of sea use. To request a larger sea area in regional planning or for individual projects, the applicants often overstate their development goals or sea-use needs. In the latter case, there are no effective standards for reviewing or for follow-up supervision and management.

(5) The punishments for illegal reclamation are inadequate. Once land reclamation is carried out, it is difficult to restore the natural state of the original sea area. To punish someone who intentionally carries out large-scale coastal reclamation activities without proper authorization, economic penalties are the most commonly used response since the reclaimed land is beyond restoration. However, according to the relevant laws and regulations, the extent of economic punishment only accounts for a small part of the profits from reclamation, and there is considerable resistance to the enforcement of the punishment for projects carried out under the instructions of local governments.

Therefore, although China's current sea-area management policies have been improved, the management of coastal reclamation and special use of the sea is still relatively loose, providing opportunities for large-scale, extensive reclamation activities.

2.5 The Outlook for the Demand of Large-Scale Coastal Reclamation Activities in China

The period of the 13th Five-Year Plan is critical for China in transforming its model of economic development. In the whole process of promoting economic and social development, and in all sectors, the government authorities must satisfy three basic requirements for the transformation.

First, the authorities responsible for marine administration are not an exception. By leveraging the construction of a society that is energy efficient and environmentally friendly, they will control the area of coastal reclamation strictly according to the principles of appropriate constraint, intensive utilization, protection of ecosystems, and comprehensive planning for the land and sea. They will improve the relevant policies to safeguard and improve people's livelihoods, particularly the legitimate rights and interests of those who use the sea for aquaculture. For better management of coastal reclamation, they will also adopt measures in such areas as project reviews, market-based allocation, coordination, enhanced supervision, and the construction of a robust legal framework.

Second, under the background of the most comprehensive and strict farmland protection system and the most rigorous measures for saving land, the trend of rapid urban development will be halted.

Third, China has become increasingly restrained in terms of its resources and environmental capacity. Heavy industries, which consume an enormous quantity of energy, inputs, and land, will grow at a much lower rate, thus alleviating the pressure on land resources.

Changes in these three dimensions will reduce the demands for coastal reclamation.

In light of the experiences of Japan, South Korea, and other countries, the rapid growth of coastal reclamation activities in the stage of rapid urban and industrial development will slow in the post-urbanization and post-industrialization stages. The steel and petroleum industries that concentrated in China's coastal areas and that made had considerable demands for coastal reclamation may soon have to face the reality of oversupply after a large-scale investment. At that point, the number of new projects will decrease, reducing the demand for coastal reclamation. Coastal ports are not only the main industrial sector occupying the coastline and sea areas but also the booster of demands for coastal reclamation. After another five years of large-scale construction, the problem of excess capacity of coastal ports will also be obvious, so the demand for coastal reclamation is expected to decrease.

In terms of the cost of reclamation, the large projects in China have for a long time been in sea areas highly suited to coastal reclamation, such as those with high beaches, low beaches, and bays. Since the turn of the 21st century, the areas suitable for such projects have become increasingly scarce. The cost of coastal reclamation will increase as projects become more difficult, the water depth increases, and more materials are needed. The cost will also rise because of higher expenditures in human capital, filling materials, and fuels. Besides, with increased contradictions between the various sea-use activities, the compensation paid for damage to the ecosystem and to relevant stakeholders will be higher.

In light of the above analysis of the overall development trend in the national economy, the social demand for reclamation, the natural conditions of reclamation, and relevant countries' experience, China's large-scale reclamation is expected to gradually slow in the future.

Chapter 3

Guideline Indicators for Designing Regional Construction Sea-Use Planning

3.1 Guideline Indicators for Designing the Regional Construction Sea-Use Planning of Ports and Piers Category

In China, a large area of the sea is used by ports and piers. These sea areas can be categorized according to their functions as port, waterway, and anchorage areas. The port areas can be further broken down into sea areas occupied by harbor basins, storage yards, operating platforms for loading and unloading, cargo transportation roads, and auxiliary facilities (Baiqiong Liu *et al.*, 2015). The ports and piers are generally located along the shoreline and project from the land out to sea. For such structures, the following factors related to intensive, ecological sea use should be considered in the design phase:

(a) intensity of coastal reclamation;
(b) changes to the shoreline;
(c) intensity of investment;
(d) efficacy of the deepwater shoreline;
(e) proportion of ecological compensation;
(f) water-environment quality in the harbor basin.

Primary guideline and assessment indicators include:

(a) an index for measuring the intensity of coastal reclamation;
(b) an index for shoreline gain or loss;
(c) an index for the intensity of investment in a sea area;
(d) an index for the intensity of investment in a shoreline section;
(e) an efficacy index for the deepwater shoreline;
(f) a net loss index for coastal wetlands;
(g) an index for the quality of the water environment.

The calculation of the indexes and the grading of their results are discussed in detail as follows.

3.1.1 *Index for the Intensity of Coastal Reclamation*

The index for the intensity of coastal reclamation is used to represent the area of the projects within a section of shoreline and how they are concentrated. It can promote the intensive use of space created by coastal reclamation and minimize the use of and damage to the original shoreline (Kai Jia, 2012). As shown in the following equation, the index for the intensity of coastal reclamation is defined as the area of coastal reclamation (hm^2) within a unit length of the shoreline (km):

$$I = \frac{S}{L}, \tag{3.1}$$

where I is the index for the intensity of coastal reclamation, S denotes the total area of coastal reclamation as envisaged in the regional sea-use plans for construction projects (ports and piers category) in hectares, and L denotes the length of shoreline in kilometers occupied by the coastal reclamation projects in the plans.

The results of the index for the intensity of coastal reclamation can be graded as follows. The results for which I is less than 50 belong to Grade I, indicating that the intensity as planned is extremely low and that measures to promote frugal and intensive use of the shoreline should be adopted. The value assigned to this grade is 0.20. The results for which I is equal to or greater than 50 but less than 100 belong to Grade II, indicating that the intensity is low and that measures for frugal and intensive use of the shoreline need to be implemented. The value assigned to this grade is 0.40. The results for which I is equal to or greater than 100 but less than

Table 3.1 Grades and values assigned using the index for the intensity of coastal reclamation.

I result (hectares per kilometer)	Grade of intensity	Definition	Value assigned
<50.0	I	The intensity of coastal reclamation is extremely low, and measures to promote frugal and intensive use of the shoreline should be adopted	0.20
50.0–100.0	II	The intensity of coastal reclamation is low, and measures for frugal and intensive use of the shoreline need to be implemented	0.40
100.0–200.0	III	The intensity of coastal reclamation is moderate, and frugal and intensive use of the shoreline needs to be maintained	0.60
200.0–300.0	IV	The intensity of coastal reclamation is high, and measures for frugal and intensive use of the reclaimed land need to be implemented	0.80
≥300.0	V	The intensity of coastal reclamation is very high, and measures to promote frugal and intensive use of the reclaimed land should be adopted	1.00

200 belong to Grade III, indicating a moderate intensity and the need to maintain frugal and intensive use of the shoreline and the reclaimed land. The value assigned to this grade is 0.60. The results for which *I* is equal to or greater than 200 but less than 300 belong to Grade IV, indicating that the intensity is high, the coastal reclamation project are rather concentrated, and the shoreline is used frugally and intensively. The value assigned to this grade is 0.80. The results for which *I* is equal to or greater than 300 can be categorized as Grade V. This grade, assigned the value of 1.00, has an intensity level that is very high, with highly concentrated coastal reclamation projects and a shoreline that is used very frugally and intensively. Table 3.1 summarizes the grades and values assigned using the index for the intensity of coastal reclamation.

3.1.2 *Index for Shoreline Gain or Loss*

The index for shoreline gain or loss is used to represent changes in shoreline length due to coastal reclamation activities (Anning Suo *et al.*, 2012c). It can be used to encourage the extension of artificial shoreline length in coastal reclamation and to minimize the use of and damage to the original shoreline. As shown in the following equation, the index for shoreline gain or loss is defined as the ratio of the total length of artificial shoreline created by coastal reclamation activities to the original shoreline length occupied:

$$R = \frac{L_n}{L_0},$$
(3.2)

where R is the index for shoreline gain or loss, L_n denotes the length of artificial shoreline in kilometers created by coastal reclamation activities as envisaged in the regional sea-use plans for construction projects (ports and piers category), and L_0 denotes the length of the original shoreline in kilometers occupied by the coastal reclamation activities.

The results of the index for shoreline gain or loss can be graded as follows. The results for which R is less than 1.0 belong to Grade I, indicating that the coastal reclamation activities as planned shorten the shoreline length. The value assigned to this grade is 0.20. The results for which R is equal to or greater than 1.00, but less than 1.20 belong to Grade II, indicating that the coastal reclamation activities as planned would increase the shoreline length to a moderate extent. The value assigned to this grade is 0.40. The results for which R is equal to or greater than 1.20 but less than 1.50 belong to Grade III, indicating a slightly extensive increase in the shoreline length. The value assigned to this grade is 0.60. The results for which R is equal to or greater than 1.50, but less than 3.00 belong to Grade IV, indicating a more than slightly extensive increase in the length of shoreline. The value assigned to this grade is 0.80. The results for which R is equal to or greater than 3.00 can be categorized as Grade V. This grade, assigned the value of 1.00, indicates a highly extensive increase in the length of the shoreline. Table 3.2 summarizes the grades and values assigned using the index for shoreline gain or loss.

3.1.3 *Index for the Intensity of Investment in Unit Sea Area*

The index for the intensity of investment in a sea area is constructed to promote intensive use of sea-area resources and to prevent extensive sea use with a low level of investment intensity. It provides a theoretical and

Table 3.2   Grades and values assigned using the index for shoreline gain or loss due to coastal reclamation.

R result	Grade of gain or loss	Definition	Value assigned
<1.0	I	Coastal reclamation activities shorten the shoreline length and lead to the loss of shoreline resources	0.20
1.0–1.20	II	Coastal reclamation activities increase the shoreline length to a moderate extent	0.40
1.20–1.50	III	Coastal reclamation activities lead to a slightly extensive increase in shoreline length	0.60
1.50–3.0	IV	Coastal reclamation activities lead to a more than slightly extensive increase in shoreline length	0.80
≥3.0	V	Coastal reclamation activities lead to a highly extensive increase in shoreline length	1.00

technical criterion for judging whether the area of land to be reclaimed according to the regional sea-use plans for construction projects (ports and piers category) is appropriate. In 2012, the SOA's Department of Sea Area Management began to use an "indicator for controlling sea-use for industrial purposes." Using surveys and research, the Department set an investment intensity criterion of 22.3864 million Yuan per hectare of sea area for major ports and piers. On the basis of this criterion, we have constructed an index for the intensity of investment for sea-area units. The index is calculated as shown in the following equation:

$$JY_i = \frac{t_{ij}}{a_{ij} \times AT_{j0}}, \tag{3.3}$$

where JY_i is the index for the intensity of investment in a unit area of the sea for Project i, t_{ij} denotes the total investment of Project i in Industry j in 10,000 Yuan, a_{ij} denotes the area of the sea used by Project i in Industry j in hectares, and AT_{j0} denotes the criterion of investment intensity in relation to the area of sea use in Industry j.

The results of the index for intensity of investment in relation to sea areas can be graded as follows. The results for which JY_i is less than 0.50 belong to Grade I of intensive sea use, with a value assigned to this

Table 3.3 Grades and values assigned using the index for the intensity of investment in sea-area units.

JY result (10,000 Yuan per hectare)	Grade of investment intensity	Definition	Value assigned
<0.50	I	The investment intensity is very low	0.20
0.50–0.80	II	The investment intensity is low	0.40
0.80–1.00	III	The investment intensity is moderate	0.60
1.00–3.00	IV	The investment intensity is high	0.80
≥3.0	V	The investment intensity is very high	1.00

grade of 0.20. The results for which JY_i is equal to or greater than 0.50 but less than 0.80 belong to Grade II, with a value assignment of 0.40. The results for which JY_i is equal to or greater than 0.80 but less than 1.00 belong to Grade III, with a value assignment of 0.60. The results for which JY_i is equal to or greater than 1.00 but less than 3.00 belong to Grade IV, with a value of 0.80. The results for which JY_i is equal to or greater than 3.00 can be categorized as Grade V, with a value assignment of 1.00. Table 3.3 summarizes the grades and values assigned using the index for the intensity of investment in sea-area units.

3.1.4 *Index for the Intensity of Investment in a Shoreline Section*

The shoreline is not only critical to the development of coastal industries but also an important strip that joins two ecological systems. Thus, intensive use of the shoreline may increase economic output through the development of shoreline resources and also affect the preservation of the shoreline's ecological functions (Baiqiong Liu *et al.*, 2014). In terms of the characteristics of sea use and shoreline use by various industries, the use of the shoreline by ports and piers can be classified as functional. That is to say, ports and piers are facilities developed on the shoreline to fulfill certain functions in the sea area. To represent the degree of intensive use of the shoreline as planned in the regional sea-use plans for construction projects (ports and piers category), we have constructed an index for the intensity of investment in unit lengths of shoreline, calculated as shown in the following equation:

$$CY_i = \frac{t_{ij}}{l_{ij} \times CT_{j0}},\tag{3.4}$$

where CY_i is the index for the intensity of investment in a shoreline section for Project i, t_{ij} denotes the total investment of Project i in Industry j in 10,000 Yuan, l_{ij} denotes the length of shoreline in kilometers occupied by Project i in Industry j, and CT_{j0} denotes the criterion of investment intensity in relation to the length of shoreline use for port and pier projects in Industry j.

In 2012, the SOA's Department of Sea Area Management developed an "indicator for controlling sea-use for industrial purposes." Using surveys and research, the Department set an investment intensity criterion of 833.3333 million Yuan per kilometer of shoreline for major ports and piers. The results of the index for the intensity of investment in relation to shoreline length can be graded as follows. The results for which CY_i is less than 0.50 belong to Grade I of intensive shorelineuse; the value assigned to this grade is 0.20. The results for which CY_i is equal to or greater than 0.50 but less than 0.80 belong to Grade II, with a value assignment of 0.40. The results for which CY_i is equal to or greater than 0.80, but less than 1.00 belong to Grade III, with a value assignment of 0.60. The results for which CY_i is equal to or greater than 1.00 but less than 3.00 belong to Grade IV, with a value assignment of 0.80. The results for which CY_i is equal to or greater than 3.00 belong to Grade V, with a value assignment of 1.00. Table 3.4 summarizes the grades and values assigned using the index for the intensity of investment in a unit length of the shoreline.

Table 3.4 Grades and values assigned using the index for the intensity of investment in a unit length of shoreline.

CY result (10,000 Yuan per kilometer)	Grade of investment intensity	Definition	Value assigned
<0.50	I	The investment intensity is very low	0.20
0.50–0.80	II	The investment intensity is low	0.40
0.80–1.00	III	The investment intensity is moderate	0.60
1.00–3.00	IV	The investment intensity is high	0.80
≥3.0	V	The investment intensity is very high	1.00

3.1.5 *Efficacy Index for the Deepwater Shoreline*

We have constructed an efficacy index for the deepwater shoreline to represent the use efficacy of the deepwater shoreline as envisaged in the regional sea-use plans for construction projects (ports and piers category). The index may be used to promote the intensive and efficient use of the deepwater shoreline and increase the economic output from its development. According to the following equations, the index can be calculated as the annual cargo throughput for a unit length of port and pier shoreline or as the economic output per unit length:

$$U_n = \frac{T_0}{L_n}, \tag{3.5}$$

$$V_n = \frac{Z_0}{L_n}, \tag{3.6}$$

where U_n represents the efficacy of use of the deepwater shoreline, T_0 denotes the annual cargo throughput in 10,000 tons as envisaged in the regional sea-use plans for construction projects (ports and piers category), L_n denotes the total length of the deepwater shoreline in kilometers occupied according to the plans, V_n denotes the capacity index for the deepwater shoreline, and Z_0 denotes the annual output in Yuan as envisaged in the plans.

The results of the efficacy index for the deepwater shoreline can be graded according to the efficacy or capacity of use of the deepwater shoreline for ports and piers as follows. The results for which the deepwater shoreline efficacy, U_n is less than 2,000.00 belong to Grade I, indicating that the planned efficacy is extremely low and that measures to promote intensive use of the shoreline should be adopted. The value assigned to this grade is 0.20. Results for which U_n is equal to or greater than 2,000.00 but less than 5,000.00 belong to Grade II, indicating that the efficacy is low and that measures for intensive use of the shoreline need to be implemented. The value assigned to this grade is 0.40. The results for which U_n is equal to or greater than 5,000.00, but less than 10,000.00 belong to Grade III, indicating a moderate efficacy. The value assigned to this grade is 0.60. The results for which U_n is equal to or greater than 10,000.00 but less than 15,000.00 belong to Grade IV,

Table 3.5 Grades and values assigned using the efficacy index for the deepwater shoreline for ports and piers.

U_n result (10,000 tons per kilometer)	Grade of usage	Definition	Value assigned
<2,000.00	I	The efficacy of use of the deepwater shoreline is very low	0.20
2,000.00–5,000.00	II	The efficacy of use of the deepwater shoreline is low	0.40
5,000.00–10,000.00	III	The efficacy of use of the deepwater shoreline is moderate	0.60
10,000.00–15,000.00	IV	The efficacy of use of the deepwater shoreline is high	0.80
≥15,000.00	V	The efficacy of use of the deepwater shoreline is very high	1.00

indicating that the efficacy is high. The value assigned to this grade is 0.80. The results for which U_n is equal to or greater than 15,000.00 belong to Grade V. This grade, being assigned the value of 1.00, indicates very high efficacy. Table 3.5 summarizes the grades and values assigned using the efficacy index for the deepwater shoreline for ports and piers.

3.1.6 *Net Loss Index for Coastal Wetlands*

In the construction of ports and piers along the shoreline and projecting out to sea, the filling, occupation, or excavation of coastal wetlands is often unavoidable. To preserve the ecological functions of coastal wetlands and minimize the occupation and damage caused by the construction of ports and piers, China could learn from the United States' experience in recent years with mitigation banks (Jingmei Li and Liu Tieying, 2012a). Specifically, all the sea-use projects for constructing ports and piers should be required to minimize the occupation of coastal wetlands. For those that have to occupy coastal wetlands, the project owner must re-create coastal wetlands of the same area adjacent to the project site to ensure that the coastal wetlands are not reduced in the region. The net loss index for coastal wetlands is used to represent the extent to which the coastal wetlands are occupied and compensated when designing regional sea-use plans for construction projects (ports and piers category) (Guoyi Wen *et al.*, 2015). It could enhance the management of occupation, damage, and compensatory mitigation of coastal wetlands and preserve the ecological functions of the shoreline. The index is calculated as shown in the following equation:

$$WD = \frac{S_t + S_w - A_t - A_w}{S_t + S_w},$$ (3.7)

where *WD* is the net loss index for coastal wetlands, S_t denotes the area of intertidal wetlands occupied or damaged by the ports and piers envisaged in the regional sea-use plans for construction projects, S_w denotes the area of wetlands between the extremely low water spring tide and −6.0 m is occupied or damaged by the ports and piers, A_t denotes the area of intertidal wetlands to be restored or re-created as envisaged in the regional sea-use plans, and A_w denotes the area of wetlands between the extremely low water spring tide and the −6.0 m isobath to be restored or re-created according to the plans.

The results of the net loss index for coastal wetlands can be graded as follows. The results for which *WD* is less than 0.20 indicate that with a majority of the wetlands occupied and damaged by the regional sea-use plans for construction projects (ports and piers category) being compensated for ecologically, the net loss of coastal wetlands is minimal. The value assigned to this grade is 1.00. The results for which *WD* is equal to or greater than 0.20 but less than 0.40 indicate that a large portion of the occupied and damaged coastal wetlands would be compensated for, and the net loss is on the low side of moderate. The value assigned to this grade is 0.80. The results for which *WD* is equal to or greater than 0.40 but less than 0.60 indicates a high compensation rate and a moderate net loss. The value assigned to this grade is 0.60. The results for which *WD* is equal to or greater than 0.60 but less than 0.80 indicate that the compensation rate is low and the net loss is considerable. The value assigned to this grade is 0.40. The results for which *WD* is equal to or greater than 0.80 indicate that the compensation rate is very low and the net loss is heavy. The value assigned to this grade is 0.20. Table 3.6 summarizes the grades and values assigned using the net loss index for coastal wetlands.

Table 3.6 Grades and values assigned using the net loss index for coastal wetlands.

WD result	Grade	Definition	Value assigned
<0.20	I	A majority of the occupied and damaged wetlands would be compensated for ecologically, and the net loss of coastal wetlands is slightly minimal	1.00
0.20–0.40	II	A large portion of the wetlands would be compensated for, and the net loss of coastal wetlands is on the low side of moderate	0.80
0.40–0.60	III	A considerable portion of the wetlands would be compensated for, and the net loss of coastal wetlands is moderate	0.60
0.60–0.80	IV	The compensation rate is low, and the net loss is considerable	0.40
≥0.80	V	The compensation rate is very low, and the net loss is heavy	0.20

3.1.7 *Index for the Quality of the Water Environment*

As a result of frequent passaging, docking, and handling operations in water areas near ports and piers, effluents from ships, cargo dropped during handling operations, and oil pollution from ships can have adverse effects on the marine ecology and landscape (Dahai Liu *et al.*, 2006; Guozhu Huang *et al.*, 2013). To preserve these and ensure the eco-friendly operation of ports and piers, we use an index for the quality of the water environment to capture the quality level and its duration. The index can be calculated as follows:

$$Q = \frac{1}{n} \sum_{i=1}^{n} \frac{dN_i}{365 N_{i0}}, \tag{3.8}$$

where Q is the index for the quality of the water environment, N_i is the measured concentration of the ith pollutant, N_{i0} denotes the category 3 water-quality standard for the ith pollutant considered by the regional sea-use plans for construction projects (ports and piers category), n denotes the number of pollutant types to be monitored and assessed, and d denotes the number of days in a year for a specific concentration of the pollutant.

Table 3.7 Grades and values assigned using the index for the quality of the water environment.

Q result	Grade	Definition	Value assigned
<0.05	I	The water-environment quality is excellent	0.20
0.15–0.05	II	The water-environment quality is good	0.40
0.15–0.25	III	The water-environment quality is satisfactory	0.60
0.25–0.35	IV	The water-environment quality is poor	0.80
≥0.35	V	The water-environment quality is terrible	1.00

The results of the index for the quality of the water environment can be graded as follows. The results for which Q is less than 0.05 belong to Grade I, which indicates that the water-environment quality in the water area covered by the regional sea-use plans for construction projects (ports and piers category) is excellent and the adverse impact from ship passaging, docking, and loading/unloading is minimal. The value assigned to this grade is 0.20. The results for which Q is equal to or greater than 0.05 but less than 0.15 belong to Grade II, indicating that the quality is good and the adverse impact is low. The value assigned to this grade is 0.40. The results for which Q is equal to or greater than 0.15 but less than 0.25 belong to Grade III, indicating a satisfactory water-environment quality and a limited adverse impact. The value assigned to this grade is 0.60. The results for which Q is equal to or greater than 0.25 but less than 0.35 belong to Grade IV, indicating that the quality is poor and the impact is considerable. The value assigned to this grade is 0.80. The results for which Q is equal to or greater than 0.35 belong to Grade V. This grade, assigned a value of 1.00, indicates that the quality is terrible and the impact is substantial. Table 3.7 summarizes the grades and values assigned using the index for the quality of the water environment.

3.2 Guideline Indicators for Designing the Regional Construction Sea-Use Planning of Coastal Industries Category

Coastal industries can be defined as industrial facilities built near the sea and ports. The regional sea-use plans for construction projects with a focus on coastal industries aim to develop coastal industries by building coastal industrial zones on reclaimed land (Chengwu Lou and Chang

Ailian, 2010). Coastal industries mainly consist of steel, petroleum refinery, shipbuilding and repairing, and coal-powered thermal plants. For intensive and ecological use of the sea by coastal industries, the following factors should be considered:

(a) intensive and frugal use of sea-area resources;
(b) intensive and frugal use of shoreline resources;
(c) occupation of coastal wetlands and ecological compensation;
(d) the proportion of production, living, and ecological spaces;
(e) the ratio of recycled wastewater;
(f) the setting of the threshold for new entrants;
(g) the quality of the water environment in adjacent sea areas.

Primary guideline and assessment indicators include:

(a) an index for the intensity of coastal reclamation;
(b) an index for the intensity of investment in sea areas;
(c) an index for marine economic output;
(d) an index for water use and effluents;
(e) an index for land used for production, living, and ecological purposes;
(f) a net loss index for wetlands;
(g) an index for the quality of the water environment;
(h) an industrial threshold index.

For the calculation of the index for the intensity of coastal reclamation, the index for the intensity of investment in sea areas, the net loss index for wetlands, and the index for the quality of the water environment, please refer to the same guideline indicators for ports and piers. The remaining part of this section will discuss the calculation and grading of the index for water use and effluents; the index for marine economic output; the index for land used for production, living, and ecological purposes; and the industrial threshold index.

3.2.1 *Index for Water Use and Effluents*

We employ the index for water use and effluents to report the ratio of authorized effluents to the water resources used by coastal industries. It may be used to help to reduce the volume of authorized effluents, promote frugal and recycled use of water resources by coastal industries, and mitigate their effects on the marine environment. It can be calculated as follows:

$$Z = \frac{W_f}{W_j},\qquad(3.9)$$

where Z is the index for water use and effluents, W_j denotes the total annual volume of water resources consumed by coastal industries covered by the regional sea-use plans for construction projects (coastal industries category), and W_f denotes the total annual volume of authorized effluents discharged by the coastal industries.

The results of the index for water use and effluents can be graded as follows. The results for which Z is less than 0.20 belong to Grade I, indicating that the ratio of recycled water resources as conceived by the regional sea-use plans for construction projects (coastal industries category) is high and that the ratio of wastewater discharged as authorized effluents is minimal. The value assigned to this grade is 1.00. The results for which Z is equal to or greater than 0.20 but less than 0.40 belong to Grade II, indicating that the ratio of recycled water is somewhat high and that of authorized effluents is low. The value assigned to this grade is 0.80. The results for which Z is equal to or greater than 0.40 but less than 0.60 belong to Grade III, indicating a relatively low ratio of recycling and

Table 3.8 Grades and values assigned using the index for water use and effluents.

Z result	Grade of intensity	Definition	Value assigned
<0.20	I	The ratio of water recycling is high, and the ratio of discharging is minimal	1.00
0.20–0.40	II	The ratio of water recycling is somewhat high, and the ratio of discharging is low	0.80
0.40–0.60	III	The ratio of recycling is relatively low, and the ratio of discharging is high	0.60
0.60–0.80	IV	The ratio of recycling is low, and the ratio of discharging is very high	0.40
≥0.80	V	The ratio of recycling is extremely low, and the ratio of discharging is extremely high	0.20

a high ratio of discharging. The value assigned to this grade is 0.60. The results for which Z is equal to or greater than 0.60 but less than 0.80 belong to Grade IV, indicating that the ratio of recycling is low and that of discharging is very high. The value assigned to this grade is 0.40. The results for which Z is equal to or greater than 0.80 belong to Grade V. This grade, assigned the value of 0.20, indicates that the ratio of recycling is extremely low and that of discharging is extremely high. Table 3.8 summarizes the grades and values assigned using the index for water use and effluents.

3.2.2 *Index for Marine Economic Output*

The coastal industrial zones generate the majority of marine economic output. To increase the economic output from the use of sea areas and to promote intensive sea-use for industrial purposes, we use the index for marine economic output to represent the economic output from industrial operations on reclaimed land in the regional sea-use plans for construction projects (coastal industries category) (Li Yao, 2007). As shown in the following equation, the index for marine economic output is defined as the annual economic output for a unit area of reclaimed land within a coastal industrial zone:

$$HJ = \frac{\sum_{i=1}^{n} V_i}{S}, \tag{3.10}$$

where HJ is the index for marine economic output in 10,000 Yuan per hectare, V_i denotes the annual output of the ith enterprise within the coastal reclamation area conceived by the regional sea-use plans for construction projects (coastal industries category), S denotes the total area of coastal reclamation envisaged in the plans, and n denotes the number of enterprises to be located in the area according to the plans.

The results of the index for marine economic output can be graded as follows. The results for which HJ is less than 200.00 belong to Grade I, indicating that the economic output as planned is extremely low and that performance in the intensive use of the sea area is very poor. The value assigned to this grade is 0.20. The results for which HJ is equal to or greater than 200.00 but less than 1000.00 belong to Grade II, indicating that the output is low and performance is poor. The value assigned to this grade is 0.40. The results for which HJ is equal to or greater than

Table 3.9   Grades and values assigned using the index for marine economic output.

HJ result	Grade	Definition	Value assigned
<200.00	I	The economic output from coastal reclamation is extremely low, and performance in the intensive use of the sea area is very poor	0.20
200.00–1,000	II	The economic output is somewhat low, and performance is relatively poor	0.40
1,000–3,000	III	The economic output is somewhat high, and performance is relatively good	0.60
3,000–5,000	IV	The economic output is high, and performance is good	0.80
≥5,000	V	The economic output is very high, and performance is very good	1.00

1,000.00 but less than 3,000.00 belong to Grade III, indicating a somewhat high output and good performance. The value assigned to this grade is 0.60. The results for which *HJ* is equal to or greater than 3,000.00 but less than 5,000.00 belong to Grade IV, indicating that the output is high and performance is good. The value assigned to this grade is 0.80. The results for which *HJ* is equal to or greater than 5,000.00 can be categorized as Grade V. This grade, assigned the value of 1.00, indicates that the output is very high and performance is very good. Table 3.9 summarizes the grades and values assigned using the index for marine economic output.

3.2.3 *Index for Land Used for Production, Living, and Ecological Purposes*

To increase industrial production, provide a well-serviced community for workers, and preserve the ecological system within the zones, it is critical that appropriate proportions of land in the coastal industrial areas be used for production, living, and ecological purposes. To determine such proportions, we use the index for land used for production, living, and ecological purposes. The land used for production includes the land occupied by the plants, storage yards, and open production sites of various enterprises. The land used for living includes residential zones, commercial zones, roads, hospitals, schools, cultural and entertainment facilities, and infrastructure. The ecological land encompasses land for vegetation, forest, wetlands, and water as part of a beautiful landscape (Benrong Peng *et al.*, 2005). The index can be calculated thus:

$$SS = \frac{SC}{S_0} : \frac{SH}{S_0} : \frac{ST}{S_0},$$
(3.11)

where *SS* represents the index, S_0 denotes the total area of coastal reclamation envisaged in the regional sea-use plans for construction projects (coastal industries category), *SC* is the area of land for production, *SH* is the area of land for living purposes, and *ST* is the area of ecological land. According to the guidelines, *SS* should be 2:1:1. The results for which *SS* is greater than 8:1:1 indicate that the proportion of production land is excessively high while that of living and ecological land is insufficient. The value assigned to this grade is 0.40. The results for which *SS* is within the range of 8:1:1 and 3:1:1 indicate that the proportion of production land is high while that of living and ecological land is relatively low. The value assigned to this grade is 0.80. The results for which *SS* is within the range of 3:1:1 and 2:1:1 indicates a moderate proportion among the three uses, and the value assigned to this grade is 1.00. The results for which *SS* ranges from 2:1:1 to 1:1:1 indicate that the proportion of land for living and ecological use is large. The value assigned to this grade is 0.80. The results for which *SS* is between 2:1:1 and 1:2:1 indicate that the proportion of land for living use is extremely large. The value assigned to this grade is 0.60. The results for which *SS* is in the range of 2:1:1 and 1:1:2 indicate that the proportion of land for ecological use is extremely large. The value assigned to this grade is 0.40. Table 3.10 summarizes the grades and values assigned using the index.

3.2.4 *Industrial Threshold Index*

We use the industrial threshold index to represent, within the scope covered by the regional sea-use plans for construction projects, the proportions of the enterprises listed in the industries prohibited or limited by national policies (Min Chu and Wangchen Liangzi, 2011). The index can help limit the enterprises that consume excessive energy, produce high pollution, and involve elevated risks in coastal areas; promote the

Table 3.10 Grades and values assigned using the index for land used for production, living, and ecological purposes.

SS result	Grade of investment intensity	Definition	Value assigned
>8:1:1	I	The proportion of production land is excessively high while that of living and ecological land is insufficient	0.40
8:1:1 to 3:1:1	II	The proportion of production land is high while that of living and ecological land is relatively low	0.80
3:1:1 to 2:1:1	III	The proportion is moderate for the three uses	1.00
2:1:1 to 1:1:1	IV	The proportion of land for living and ecological use is large	0.80
2:1:1 to 1:2:1	V	The proportion of land for living use is extremely large	0.60
2:1:1 to 1:1:2	VI	The proportion of land for ecological use is extremely large	0.40

structural optimization of coastal industries as soon as possible; and enhance production efficacy. The index is calculated as shown in the following equation:

$$CM = \frac{\sum_{j=1}^{m} U_j}{\sum_{i=1}^{n} V_i},\qquad(3.12)$$

where CM is the industrial threshold index, V_i denotes the output of the ith enterprise covered by the regional sea-use plans for construction projects (coastal industries category), U_j denotes the output of the jth enterprise covered by the plans and belonging to an industry prohibited or limited by national policies, n denotes the number of enterprises to be located in an area according to the plans, and m denotes the number of enterprises covered by the plans and belonging to an industry prohibited or limited by national policies.

For the list of industries prohibited or limited by national policies, please refer to the *Inventory of Industries Prohibited or Limited by National Policies*. The results of the industrial threshold index can be graded as follows. The results for which CM is greater than 0.80 belong to Grade I,

Table 3.11   Grades and values assigned using the industrial threshold index.

CM result	Grade	Definition	Value assigned
>0.80	I	The proportion of enterprises belonging to industries prohibited or limited by national policies is extremely high	0.20
0.60–0.80	II	The proportion of enterprises belonging to industries prohibited or limited by national policies is very high	0.40
0.40–0.60	III	The proportion of enterprises belonging to industries prohibited or limited by national policies is high	0.60
0.20–0.40	IV	The proportion of enterprises belonging to industries prohibited or limited by national policies is relatively high	0.80
≤0.20	V	The proportion of enterprises belonging to industries prohibited or limited by national policies is relatively low	1.00

indicating that the proportion of enterprises belonging to industries prohibited or limited by national policies is extremely high. The value assigned to this grade is 0.20. The results for which *CM* is greater than 0.60 but less than or equal to 0.80 belong to Grade II, indicating that the proportion is very high. The value assigned to this grade is 0.40. The results for which *CM* is greater than 0.40 but less than or equal to 0.60 belong to Grade III, indicating that the proportion is high. The value assigned to this grade is 0.60. The results for which *CM* is greater than 0.20 but less than or equal to 0.40 belong to Grade IV, indicating that the proportion is relatively high. The value assigned to this grade is 0.80. The results for which *CM* is less than 0.20 belong to Grade V. This grade, assigned the value of 1.00, indicates that the proportion is relatively low. Table 3.11 summarizes the grades and values assigned using the industrial threshold index.

3.3 Guideline Indicators for Designing the Regional Construction Sea-Use Planning of Coastal Towns Category

In China, the use of sea areas to build coastal towns is a new and promising kind of sea use. When building these towns, it is critical to mandate and promote intensive and ecological sea use in order to beautify the shoreline and meet the requirements imposed by China's marine ecological civilization strategies. The regional sea-use plans for construction projects (coastal towns category) focus on the building and development of coastal towns. In these plans, coastal reclamation is the primary way of expanding urban development space to build commercial and residential zones such as coastal cities, towns, and districts (Xiang Lan, 2009a). For the most part, the following factors should be considered in designing the plans:

(a) intensive and frugal use of sea-area resources;
(b) intensive and frugal use of shoreline resources;
(c) occupation of coastal wetlands and ecological compensation;
(d) seafront spaces and shoreline;
(e) proportion of land used for vegetation;
(f) population density;
(g) quality of the water environment in adjacent sea areas.

Primary guideline and assessment indicators include:

(a) an index for the intensity of coastal reclamation;
(b) an index for the intensity of investment in sea areas;
(c) an index for shoreline gain or loss;
(d) an index for the seafront shoreline;
(e) proportion of land used for vegetation;
(f) a net loss index for wetlands;
(g) an index for the quality of the water environment;
(h) a space per capita index;
(i) an index for waterfront zones;
(j) an index for the water landscape.

For the calculation of the index for the intensity of coastal reclamation, the index for shoreline gain or loss, the index for the intensity of investment in sea areas, the net loss index for wetlands, and the index for the quality of the water environment, please refer to the same guideline indicators for ports and piers. The remaining part of this section will discuss the calculation and grading of the index for the seafront shoreline, the index for waterfront zones, the index for the water landscape, the proportion of land used for vegetation, and the space per capita index.

3.3.1 *Index for the Seafront Shoreline*

The index for the seafront shoreline is employed to represent the construction of the seafront shoreline in coastal urban development. The index may be used to promote the extension of the shoreline and help to meet people's increasing demand for seafront or waterfront shorelines. As shown in the equation below, the index for the seafront shoreline can be calculated as the ratio of the length of the seafront shoreline added during coastal urban development to the total length of shoreline increased due to the development.

$$C_z = \frac{L_p}{L_t}, \tag{3.13}$$

where C_z is the index for the seafront shoreline, L_p denotes the length of the public seafront shoreline added in the regional sea-use plans for construction projects (coastal towns category) or the shoreline space freely accessible to the public, and L_t denotes the total length of the shoreline increased due to the plans.

The results of the index for the seafront shoreline can be graded as follows. The results for which C_z is less than 0.10 belong to Grade I, indicating that the proportion of the seafront shoreline added by the coastal urban development is minimal. It may not meet the public demand for seafront and sea view zones. The value assigned to this grade is 0.20. The results for which C_z is equal to or greater than 0.10 but less than 0.20 belong to Grade II, indicating that the proportion is relatively low and that the public demand for the seafront and sea view zones cannot be fully satisfied. The value assigned to this grade is 0.40. The results for which C_z is equal to or greater than 0.20 but less than 0.30 belong to Grade III, indicating that the proportion is high and that public demand can be satisfied. The value assigned to this grade is 0.60. The results for which C_z is equal to or greater than 0.30 but less than 0.50 belong to Grade IV, indicating that the proportion is very high and that public demand can be readily satisfied. The value assigned to this grade is 0.80. The results for which C_z is equal to or greater than 0.50 can be categorized as Grade V. This grade, assigned the value of 1.00, indicates that the proportion is extremely high and that public demand can be met to the greatest extent. Table 3.12 summarizes the grades and values assigned using the index for the seafront shoreline.

Table 3.12 Grades and values assigned using the index for the seafront shoreline in coastal towns.

C_z result	Grade of seafront proportion	Definition	Value assigned
<0.10	I	The proportion of seafront shoreline is minimal	0.20
0.10–0.20	II	The proportion of seafront shoreline is relatively low	0.40
0.20–0.30	III	The proportion of seafront shoreline is high	0.60
0.30–0.50	IV	The proportion of seafront shoreline is very high	0.80
≥0.50	V	The proportion of seafront shoreline is extremely high	1.00

3.3.2 Index for Waterfront Zones

The index for waterfront zones is used to represent the proportion of waterfront zones in coastal urban development. It may be used to facilitate the control of the cumulative effects of the large-sized development activities on the marine environment by promoting waterfront designs such as artificial islands. It may also be used to promote the formation of more waterfront land. As shown in the following equation, the index can be calculated as the proportion of the land area of the zone within 500 meters of the shoreline to the total land area obtained from coastal reclamation in coastal urban development:

$$A_c = \frac{S_{500}}{S_0},$$

(3.14)

where A_c is the index for waterfront zones, S_0 denotes the total land area in hectares obtained from coastal reclamation in coastal urban development, and S_{500} is the land area in hectares of the zone within 500 meters of the shoreline.

To characterize the proportion of the waterfront zone area, we group the results of the index for waterfront zones into five grades. The results for which A_c is less than 0.20 indicate that the proportion of the waterfront zones is minimal due to excessively large blocks of land from coastal reclamation, the tightly packed shape, and the very limited extension of shoreline length. The value assigned to this grade is 0.20.

Table 3.13   Grades and values assigned using the index for waterfront zones.

A_c result	Grade	Definition	Value assigned
<0.20	I	The proportion of the waterfront zone is minimal due to excessively large blocks of land from coastal reclamation	0.20
0.20–0.40	II	The proportion is relatively low due to large blocks of land	0.40
0.40–0.60	III	The proportion is moderate, with large block of land but greater complexity	0.60
0.60–0.80	IV	The proportion is relatively high with blocks of land of moderate area	0.80
≥0.80	V	The proportion is very high, with smaller blocks of land	1.00

The results for which A_c is equal to or greater than 0.20 but less than 0.40 indicate that the proportion is relatively low due to the large blocks of land, the relatively packed shape, and the limited extension of shoreline length. The value assigned to this grade is 0.40. The results for which A_c is equal to or greater than 0.40 but less than 0.60 indicate that the proportion is moderate, comprising large blocks of land but with the shape of the spaces becoming more complex and the length of the shoreline being extended to a certain extent. The value assigned to this grade is 0.60. The results for which A_c is equal to or greater than 0.60 but less than 0.80 indicate that the proportion is relatively high, with small blocks of land and even more complex shapes occupying the space. The value assigned to this grade is 0.80. The results for which A_c is equal to or greater than 0.80 can be categorized in the fifth grade, assigned the value of 1.00, indicating that the proportion is very high, with smaller blocks of land and very complex shapes occupying the space. Table 3.13 summarizes the grade and values assigned using the index for waterfront zones.

3.3.3 *Index for the Water Landscape*

The index for the water landscape is used to represent the area reserved for the water landscape in the regional sea-use plans for construction projects (coastal towns category). The index may be used to promote the provision of sufficient water areas in the plans. It is instrumental in the building of a waterfront and seafront environment, enhancing the effects of the water landscape in coastal urban zones and improving the local marine ecological environment. As shown in the following equation, the index can be calculated as the proportion of the area reserved for the water landscape in the plans to the total area of planned sea use:

$$A_w = \frac{S_w}{S_0},$$ (3.15)

where A_w is the index for the water landscape, S_0 denotes the total area in hectares as envisaged in the regional sea-use plans for construction projects, and S_w denotes the area reserved for the water landscape in hectares according to the plans.

The results for the index for the water landscape can be graded as follows. The results for which A_w is less than 0.05 belong to Grade I, indicating that a minimal area is reserved for the water landscape and that the seafront water area is insufficient. The value assigned to this grade is 0.20. The results for which A_w is equal to or greater than 0.05 but less than 0.15 belong to Grade II, indicating that the area reserved is relatively small and that the seafront water area is somewhat insufficient. The value assigned to this grade is 0.40. The results for which A_w is equal to or greater than 0.15 but less than 0.25 belong to Grade III, indicating a barely sufficient reserved area and a satisfactory seafront water area. The value assigned to this grade is 0.60. The results for which A_w is equal to or greater than 0.25 but less than 0.35 belong to Grade IV, indicating that the reserved area is sufficient and that the seafront water area is substantial. The value assigned to this grade is 0.80. The results for which A_w is equal to or greater than 0.35 can be categorized as Grade V. This grade, assigned the value of 1.00, indicates that the reserved area is quite sufficient and that the seafront water area is very substantial. Table 3.14 summarizes the grades and values assigned using the index for the water landscape.

3.3.4 *Proportion of Land Used for Vegetation*

Land for vegetation is an essential part of the new urban zones. It not only purifies the air, beautifies the environment, and preserves biodiversity but

Table 3.14 Grades and values assigned using the index for the water landscape.

A_w result	Grade	Definition	Value assigned
<0.05	I	A minimal area is reserved for the water landscape, and the seafront water area is insufficient	0.20
0.05–0.15	II	The area reserved is relatively small, and the seafront water area is just acceptable	0.40
0.15–0.25	III	The reserved area is barely sufficient, and the seafront water area is satisfactory	0.60
0.25–0.35	IV	The reserved area is sufficient, and the seafront water area is substantial	0.80
≥0.35	V	The reserved area is quite sufficient, and the seafront water area is very substantial	1.00

also offers an outdoor area for leisure, entertainment, and disaster relief. However, excessively stringent protection of land for vegetation may waste sea-area resources and involve high maintenance costs. Therefore, the proportion of land used for vegetation has become a crucial quantitative performance indicator in urban planning and construction. For this section, land used for vegetation refers to urban land that has ecological functions, including lawns, meadows, brush, forests, water areas, and wetlands. The proportion can be calculated according to the equation below.

$$LD = \frac{\sum_{i=1}^{m} U_i}{S_{\text{Total}}}, \qquad (3.16)$$

where LD is the proportion of land used for vegetation, S_{Total} denotes the total area in the regional sea-use planning for construction projects (coastal towns category); U_i is the area of the ith vegetation land, and m denotes the total number of vegetation land blocks as envisaged in the plan.

The proportion of land used for vegetation can be grouped into five grades. The results for which LD is less than 0.10 belong to Grade I, indicating that the proportion is minimal. The value assigned to this grade is 0.40. The results for which LD is equal to or greater than 0.10 but less than 0.20 belong to Grade II, indicating that the proportion is low. The value

Table 3.15 Grades and values assigned using the index for the proportion of land used for vegetation.

LD result	Grade	Definition	Value assigned
<0.10	I	The proportion of land used for vegetation is minimal	0.40
0.10–0.20	II	The proportion of land used for vegetation is low	0.60
0.20–0.40	III	The proportion of land used for vegetation is moderate	1.00
0.40–0.50	IV	The proportion of land used for vegetation is relatively high	0.60
≥0.50	V	The proportion of land used for vegetation is high	0.40

assigned to this grade is 0.60. The results for which *LD* is equal to or greater than 0.20 but less than 0.40 belong to Grade III, indicating a moderate proportion. The value assigned to this grade is 1.00. The results for which *LD* is equal to or greater than 0.40 but less than 0.50 belong to Grade IV, indicating that the proportion is relatively high. The value assigned to this grade is 0.60. The results for which *LD* is equal to or greater than 0.50 can be categorized as Grade V. This grade, assigned the value of 0.40, indicates that the proportion is high. Table 3.15 summarizes the grades and values assigned using the index for the proportion of land used for vegetation.

3.3.5 *Space per Capita Index*

The coastal towns are designed with the intention of accommodating people. Therefore, providing a suitable living environment is fundamental to the building of such towns. A moderate space per capita is vital for a suitable living environment. The space per capita index is a useful tool for controlling the area of the coastal towns. In this section, space per capita is used to represent suitability in terms of environment and area as envisaged by the regional sea-use plans for construction projects (coastal towns category) (Siliang Hu, 2011). As shown in the equation below, space per capita is simply the ratio of the total population to the total area indicated in the plans.

$$RJ = \frac{P_{\text{Total}}}{S_{\text{Total}}}, \tag{3.17}$$

where *RJ* is the space per capita in persons per hectare, S_{Total} denotes the total area in the regional sea-use plans for construction projects (coastal

Table 3.16 Grades and values assigned using the space per capita index.

RJ (persons/hm²)	Grade	Definition	Value assigned
<50.00	I	The town size is excessively large, and only a few people live in the town	0.40
50.00–100.00	II	The town is relatively large, with a sparse population	0.60
100.00–150.00	III	The size of both the town and population is moderate	1.00
150.00–200.00	IV	The town is packed, with a large population	0.80
≥200.00	V	The town is highly packed, with a dense population	0.60

towns category), and P_{Total} denotes the total population indicated in the plans.

The results of the space per capita index can be graded as follows. The results for which RJ is less than 50 belong to Grade I, indicating that the town size is excessively large and that only a few people live in the town. The value assigned to this grade is 0.40. The results for which RJ is equal to or greater than 50 but less than 100 belong to Grade II, indicating that the town is relatively large with a sparse population. The value assigned to this grade is 0.60. The results for which RJ is equal to or greater than 100 but less than 150 belong to Grade III, indicating a moderate size of both town and population. The value assigned to this grade is 1.00. The results for which RJ is equal to or greater than 150 but less than 200 belong to Grade IV, indicating that the town is packed, with a large population. The value assigned to this grade is 0.80. The results for which RJ is equal to or greater than 200 can be categorized as Grade V. This grade, assigned the value of 0.60, indicates that the town is highly packed, with a dense population. Table 3.16 summarizes the grades and values assigned using the space per capita index.

3.4 Guideline Indicators for Designing the Regional Construction Sea-Use Planning of Tourism and Entertainment Facilities Category

Sea use for tourism, leisure, and entertainment is a new way of developing marine tourism resources and boosting the marine economy. With the area of the sea used for tourism, leisure, and entertainment increasing rapidly in recent years, the number of regional sea-use plans for construction projects in this category has also increased. The design of plans for this category should take into account the following factors:

(a) intensive and frugal use of sea-area resources;
(b) intensive and frugal use of shoreline resources;
(c) occupation of coastal wetlands and ecological compensation;
(d) seafront spaces and shoreline;
(e) landscape diversity and entertainment program variety;
(f) proportion of tourism infrastructure to be built;
(g) the quality of the water environment in adjacent sea areas.

Primary guideline and assessment indicators include:

(a) an index for the intensity of coastal reclamation;
(b) an index for the intensity of investment in sea areas;
(c) an index for shoreline gain or loss;
(d) an index for the seafront shoreline;
(e) an index for landscape diversity;
(f) a net loss index for wetlands;
(g) an index for the quality of the water environment;
(h) an index for entertainment program variety;
(i) an index for waterfront zones;
(j) an index for the water landscape;
(k) an index for tourism infrastructure;
(l) an index for marine passages.

For the calculation of the index for the intensity of coastal reclamation, the index for shoreline gain or loss, the index for the intensity of investment in sea areas, the net loss index for wetlands, and the index for the quality of the water environment, please refer to the same guideline indicators for the category of ports and piers. For the calculation of the index for the seafront shoreline, the index for waterfront zones, and the index for the water landscape, please refer to the same guideline indicators for the category of coastal towns. The remaining part of this section will discuss the calculation of the index for marine passages, the index for tourism infrastructure, the index for entertainment program variety, and the index for landscape diversity.

3.4.1 *Index for Marine Passages*

The index for marine passages is used to represent the consideration given to marine environmental processes in designing regional sea-use plans for construction projects (tourism and entertainment facilities category). The index aims to reduce the blocking of marine hydrodynamic processes and the migration paths of marine life, thus improving the water exchange process, increasing the seafront shoreline, and promoting the building of more offshore or island tourism, leisure, and entertainment facilities. The index is the sum of the width measured at the narrowest points on all the tidal passages reserved according to the plans. It can be calculated as per the equation as follows:

$$H_w = \sum_{i=1}^{n} W_{si}, \tag{3.18}$$

where H_w is the index for marine passages in meters and W_{si} is the width in meters measured at the narrowest point on the ith tidal passages reserved according to the plans.

The results of the index for marine passages can be graded as follows. The results for which H_w is less than 200.00 belong to Grade I, indicating that the marine process passages are too narrow to fulfill their functions properly. The value assigned to this grade is 0.20. The results for which H_w is equal to or greater than 200.00 but less than 500.00 belong to Grade II, indicating that the passages are narrow and can only fulfill limited functions. The value assigned to this grade is 0.40. The results for which H_w is equal to or greater than 500.00 but less than 1,000.00 belong to Grade III, indicating wide passages and fulfilled functions. The value assigned to this grade is 0.60. The results for which H_w is equal to or greater than 1,000.00 but less than 2,000.00 belong to Grade IV, indicating that the passages are very wide and can fulfill their functions with ease. The value assigned to this grade is 0.80. The results for which H_w is equal to or greater than 2,000.00 can be categorized as Grade V. This grade, assigned the value 1.00, indicates that the passages are extremely wide and that the functions are fulfilled extensively. Table 3.17 summarizes the grades and values assigned using the index for marine passages.

Table 3.17   Grades and values assigned using the index for marine passages.

H_w result (m)	Grade	Definition	Value assigned
<200.0	I	The passages are too narrow to fulfill their functions	0.20
200.0–500.0	II	The passages are narrow and can only fulfill limited functions	0.40
500.0–1,000.0	III	The passages are relatively wide, and the functions can be fulfilled	0.60
1,000.0–2,000.0	IV	The passages are very wide and can fulfill their functions with ease	0.80
≥2,000.0	V	The passages are extremely wide, and the functions are fulfilled extensively	1.00

3.4.2 Index for Tourism Infrastructure

The index for tourism infrastructure is used to represent the proportion of infrastructure comprising hotels and restaurants in the total area according to the regional sea-use plans for construction projects (tourism and entertainment facilities category). The index may be used to facilitate the regulation of the category and prevent coastal real estate development in the name of developing tourism, leisure, and entertainment industry. As shown in the equation below, it is the proportion of land area for building tourism infrastructure to the total area of coastal reclamation according to the plans.

$$LS = \frac{\sum_{i=1}^{n} a_i}{S_0}, \tag{3.19}$$

where LS is the index for tourism infrastructure, S_0 denotes the total area according to the plan, a_i denotes the land area for building the ith tourism infrastructure covered by the plans, and n denotes the amount of tourism infrastructure covered by the plans.

The results of the index for tourism infrastructure can be graded as follows. The results for which LS is less than 0.10 indicate that the proportion of the area of tourism infrastructure is extremely low. The value assigned to this grade is 0.40. The results for which LS is equal to or greater than 0.10 but less than 0.15 indicate that the proportion is relatively low.

Table 3.18 Grades and values assigned using the index for tourism infrastructure.

LS result	Grade	Definition	Value assigned
<0.10	I	The proportion of the area of tourism infrastructure is extremely low	0.40
0.10–0.15	II	The proportion is relatively low	0.60
0.15–0.20	III	The proportion is moderate	1.00
0.20–0.25	IV	The proportion is relatively large	0.40
≥0.25	V	The proportion is excessively large	0.20

The value assigned to this grade is 0.60. The results for which *LS* is equal to or greater than 0.15 but less than 0.20 indicate a moderate proportion. The value assigned to this grade is 1.00. The results for which *LS* is equal to or greater than 0.20 but less than 0.25 indicate that the proportion is relatively large. The value assigned to this grade is 0.40. The results for which *LS* is equal to or greater than 0.25 indicate that the proportion is excessively large, and the value assigned to this grade is 0.20. Table 3.18 summarizes the grades and values assigned using the index for tourism infrastructure.

3.4.3 *Index for Entertainment Program Variety*

The index for entertainment program variety is used to represent the level of variety in the offerings of tourism, leisure, and entertainment programs included in the regional sea-use plans for construction projects (tourism and entertainment facilities category). It aims to improve the efficacy of the plans; enhance functions in terms of tourism, leisure, and entertainment; and promote the inclusion of diversified programs in the plans. It can be calculated as per the equation as follows.

$$YL = -\sum_{i=1}^{s} g_i \ln g_i, \tag{3.20}$$

where *YL* is the index for entertainment program variety, g_i denotes the proportion of visitor capacity of the *i*th type of tourism, leisure, or entertainment zones to the total capacity of all the tourism, leisure, and entertainment facilities in the plans, and S denotes the total number of tourism, leisure, and entertainment types covered by the plans.

The results of the index for entertainment program variety can be graded as follows. The results for which YL is less than 0.10 belong to Grade I, indicating that the types of tourism, leisure, and entertainment facilities covered by the plans are monotonous and have minimal attractiveness for visitors. The value assigned to this grade is 0.20. The results for which YL is equal to or greater than 0.10 but less than 0.20 belong to Grade II, indicating that the types are somewhat monotonous and have limited attractiveness for visitors. The value assigned to this grade is 0.40. The results for which YL is equal to or greater than 0.20 but less than 0.30 belong to Grade III, indicating somewhat diverse types and a certain attractiveness for visitors. The value assigned to this grade is 0.60. The results for which YL is equal to or greater than 0.30 but less than 0.50 belong to Grade IV, indicating that the types are diverse and have a strong attractiveness for visitors. The value assigned to this grade is 0.80. The results for which YL is equal to or greater than 0.50 can be categorized as Grade V. This grade, assigned the value of 1.00, means that the types are highly diverse and have a very strong attractiveness for visitors. Table 3.19 summarizes the grades and values assigned using the index for entertainment program variety.

Table 3.19 Grades and values assigned using the index for entertainment program variety.

YL result	Grade	Definition	Value assigned
<0.10	I	The types of tourism, leisure, and entertainment facilities covered by the plans are monotonous and have minimal attractiveness for visitors	0.20
0.10–0.20	II	The types are somewhat monotonous and have limited attractiveness for visitors	0.40
0.20–0.30	III	The types are somewhat diverse and have a relatively strong attractiveness for visitors	0.60
0.30–0.50	IV	The types are diverse and have a strong attractiveness for visitors	0.80
≥0.50	V	The types are highly diverse and have a very strong attractiveness for visitors	1.00

3.4.4 *Index for Landscape Diversity*

A diverse landscape designed in the regional sea-use plans for construction projects (tourism and entertainment facilities category) can effectively enhance the performance of the landscape, increase the fun of travel, and facilitate the provision of a large variety of tourism, leisure, and entertainment activities. The index for landscape diversity is used to describe the level of diversity in the design of the landscape covered in the plans. It may enhance the level of diversity and can be calculated using the following equation:

$$D = -\sum_{i=1}^{m} p_i \ln p_i, \tag{3.21}$$

where D is the index for landscape diversity, p_i denotes the proportion of the ith landscape type to the total area as planned, and m denotes the number of landscape types covered by the plans.

The results of the index for landscape diversity can be graded as follows. The results for which D is less than 0.10 belong to Grade I, indicating that the types of landscape covered by the plans are extremely monotonous and have a minimal attractiveness for visitors. The value assigned to this grade is 0.20. The results for which D is equal to or greater

Table 3.20 Grades and values assigned using the index for landscape diversity.

D result	Grade	Definition	Value assigned
<0.10	I	The types of landscape are extremely monotonous and have minimal attractiveness for visitors	0.20
0.10–0.20	II	The types of landscape are monotonous and have limited attractiveness for visitors	0.40
0.20–0.30	III	The types of landscape are diverse and have a somewhat strong attractiveness for visitors	0.60
0.30-0.50	IV	The types of landscape are highly diverse and have a strong attractiveness for visitors	0.80
≥0.50	V	The types of landscapes are extremely diverse and have a very strong attractiveness for visitors	1.00

than 0.10 but less than 0.20 belong to Grade II, indicating that the types are monotonous and have limited attractiveness for visitors. The value assigned to this grade is 0.40. The results for which D is equal to or greater than 0.20 but less than 0.30 belong to Grade III, indicating somewhat diverse types and a certain attractiveness for visitors. The value assigned to this grade is 0.60. The results for which D is equal to or greater than 0.30 but less than 0.50 belong to Grade IV, indicating that the types are highly diverse and have a strong attractiveness for visitors. The value assigned to this grade is 0.80. The results for which D is equal to or greater than 0.50 can be categorized as Grade V. This grade, assigned the value of 1.00, indicates that the types are extremely diverse and have a very strong attractiveness for visitors. Table 3.20 summarizes the grades and values assigned using the index for landscape diversity.

Chapter 4

Plan Management for Coastal Reclamation

4.1 Overview of Plan Management for Coastal Reclamation

In China's coastal regions, coastal reclamation is an essential source of construction land, accounting for a significant share of the total area of new construction land. To control the total area of coastal reclamation activities, in 2009, the National Development and Reform Commission (NDRC) and the State Oceanic Administration (SOA) jointly issued the Notice on Strengthening the Plan Management in Planning Coastal Reclamation Projects. In particular, the Notice required annual plan management for coastal reclamation projects and imposed strict rules on Plan use. The annual plan management system is a useful tool. It can enhance the role of coastal reclamation in supporting economic development effectively, improve efficiency in sea use, facilitate the implementation of marine functional zoning, and assist with macroeconomic regulation. It is also crucial to efforts to optimize the sea area resources, promote the improvement of the land resource management system, and fine-tune the timing of land supply.

4.1.1 The Role of Coastal Reclamation in Plan Control on Construction Land

Plan control is critical to land administration; for construction land administration, in particular, it is the first checkpoint (see Figure 4.1). The Plan

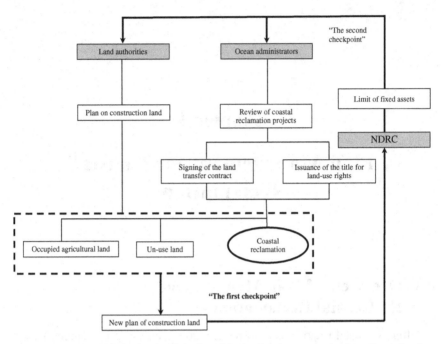

Figure 4.1 "Double checkpoints" deployed by land and ocean authorities for reviewing coastal reclamation projects.

applied to new construction land is at the core of land-use plan management and is an effective channel connecting land policies and macroeconomic regulation. As per the land administration rules currently in force, land authorities must implement the overall planning and annual Plan on land use strictly. Any new construction land must be in line with the planning and included in the calculation of the annual plan. Those that do not conform to the planning or do not have the allocated plan will not be approved. Moreover, the total area of construction land in a specific region should not exceed the plan set by the overall land-use plan at the immediate higher level. Both agricultural land requisition and undeveloped land are accounted for in calculating the plan of new construction land and the annual plan of land use, but for effective control of new construction land, in addition to the agricultural land and the undeveloped land currently available, plan management should also cover land added from coastal reclamation (Yonghai Yu and Suo Anning, 2013a).

Ocean administrators are required to set the annual plan for coastal reclamation according to the government's target of the total area of construction land and the annual plan for new construction land. They then have to allocate the plan to different regions appropriately on the basis of their sea-area conditions and the demand generated by social and economic development. The sum of the allocated plan should not exceed the annual total, which is an essential criterion in deciding whether to approve the request for sea use. With tidal flat resources included in the land planning framework for undeveloped land and subject to plan management, disorderly development may be prevented with strict control. Moreover, efforts in this area may improve the control of the total area of new construction land, enhance the effects of land plans on overall economic regulation, and close the loophole in land administration.

After a coastal reclamation project is completed, substantial investments—often several times larger than the original project investment in area—are needed to build a comprehensive infrastructure and develop real estate or industrial projects. In China, investments in fixed assets are employed as leverage for macroeconomic regulation. For its target of fixed asset investments, the NDRC should control the area of coastal reclamation rigorously.

Deciding on the annual plan of coastal reclamation involves not only identifying suitable locations but also estimating the right area and timing in line with the needs of macroeconomic regulation. Given the current system of marine functional zoning, quantitative indicators such as limits on construction land and fixed asset investment could be employed to strengthen the management of coastal reclamation. For example, in regions where investments in coastal reclamation and new projects start to increase at an exceptionally rapid rate, the indicators could be used to manage coastal reclamation and new construction land simultaneously. By strengthening the management of investments in construction projects and preventing disorderly development of sea areas, the measures' contribution to stable and moderate economic growth will come to be fully appreciated by local governments.

4.1.2 *Major Principles to be Adopted in Plan Management for Coastal Reclamation*

The plan for coastal reclamation represents the medium-term and annual arrangements made by the central or local government. Nationwide coastal reclamation management and the plan system are only effective in regulating the area of coastal reclamation, maintaining orderly market conditions, curbing disorder and excessive coastal reclamation, and safeguarding the sustainable use of sea-area resources if they are established while taking due consideration of China's basic conditions, are consistent over time, are based on science and a systematic approach, and are highly restrictive and enforceable. Therefore, the following major principles must be adopted when building a plan management system for coastal reclamation.

(1) *Keep in line with macroeconomic targets while giving priority to key projects*: In essence, annual plan management for coastal reclamation is one aspect of administrative services. It involves planning coastal reclamation activities on the basis of local conditions, including natural conditions and the characteristics of the resources in specific shoreline sections, the level of social and economic development, and macroeconomic targets. Priority should be given to construction projects under national strategies. Excessive demand should be curbed or restricted. With the capacity to optimize the locations, timing, and management of coastal reclamation, the annual Plan management system is a useful tool for the government for regulating coastal reclamation at the macro level.

(2) *Consistency and coordination*: Governments at various levels should coordinate in setting the annual Plan and limits to ensure that central and local governments take a systematic and consistent approach in annual plan management for coastal reclamation. Moreover, the demand for coastal reclamation in various sea programs should be considered comprehensively to coordinate competing interests, thereby reducing disputes and conflict in annual plan management for coastal reclamation.

(3) *Benefit maximization*: Regulators should increase public awareness that marine resources can serve different purposes and that the sea can be developed in diversified ways; they should also correct the misconception that "land reclamation from the sea can be continued indefinitely." They should promote intensive and frugal use of sea-area resources. In deciding the suitable annual area and spatial distribution of coastal reclamation projects, they should take into account the specific sea area's natural resource conditions, the state of the environment, the geographical location, previous development projects, and the social and economic development needs at the national or local level. In summary, the goal is to

maximize the use of sea-area resources for optimal social, economic, and ecological benefits.

(4) *Striking the right balance between development and conservation*: Annual plan management for coastal reclamation involves understanding how nature works. Plans for control measures on and spatial distribution of coastal reclamation activities nationwide should consider the overall value of marine resources, their ability to regenerate, and the carrying capacity of the marine environment. The Plan established should be able to meet the needs of marine economic development while allowing for effective protection of important "intact" marine areas, rare and endangered marine species and their habitats, typical marine ecosystems, representative marine natural landscapes, and natural or historical marine sites of profound value for scientific research.

(5) *Basis in scientific evidence*: The annual plan for coastal reclamation should be established on the basis of scientific assessments combined with qualitative experience, with quantitative assessments governing in case of any inconsistency between quantitative and qualitative results. The rule aims to ensure that plan management is based on comprehensive and reliable information rather than on subjective judgment.

(6) *A forward-looking approach*: Annual plan management for coastal reclamation needs to maintain sustainability in terms of marine development and protection while allowing for technological progress and future improvements. Forward-looking management is needed to fully take into consideration potential progress in science and technology as well as industrial sea-use demands in line with future social and economic development. Specifically, preventive measures should be taken in advance against inappropriate coastal reclamation activities, and adequate reserves should be set for future demands due to marine economic development.

4.2 Procedures and Rules of Plan Management for Coastal Reclamation

Plan management for coastal reclamation is based on several annual plan indicators. The indicators include not only an indicator of the area but also other supplementary indicators. Together, these form a fairly

Table 4.1   System of indicators for coastal reclamation plans.

Primary indicators	Supplementary indicators
Functional coastal reclamation	Length of shoreline occupied by functional coastal reclamation
Land reclamation	Land reclaimed per unit length of shoreline
	Percentage of the offshore area

comprehensive system of indicators (see Table 4.1). In the initial stage, it is advisable to include only a few indicators, which are open to revision or addition over time during the implementation of the plan.

Coastal reclamation needed to fulfill the functions of ports, thermal power plants, and shipping facilities is initially defined as functional coastal reclamation (as distinct from the land designated for industrial or mining use in inland programs). The supplementary indicator is the length of shoreline occupied by functional coastal reclamation. The acquisition of land from encircling a sea area to build industrial or urban zones is defined as land reclamation. Its supplementary indicators are the land reclaimed per unit length of shoreline and percentage of offshore area. All the indicators are used to manage added plans for coastal reclamation.

4.2.1 *Setting the Values of Coastal Reclamation Plan Indicators*

The plan for coastal reclamation is set centrally and administered by authorities at various levels. Specifically, the NDRC and SOA are responsible for the setting and administration of national Plans for coastal reclamation. The development and reform authorities, as well as the ocean administrators of coastal provinces (including autonomous regions and municipalities directly under the central government), are responsible for suggesting the value of the coastal reclamation plan indicators and their administration for the administrative regions at their corresponding level. The suggested value of coastal reclamation plan indicators (for coastal reclamation for both construction and agricultural purposes) for an administrative region is estimated jointly by the ocean administrator and the development and reform authority of the coastal province (or the autonomous region or municipality directly under the central government) in line with local marine functional zoning, the characteristics of sea area resources, the current state of the ecological environment, and the demand for economic and social development. The estimated value should be submitted to the SOA and NDRC as required. In the suggestions submitted by the provincial authorities, the value for some major cities should be presented separately. The SOA will propose the national values of the coastal reclamation plan indicators and, after consultation with the relevant authorities, will recommend how the value should be allocated to different provinces, basing its recommendation on the submitted suggestions, the marine functional zoning, the coastal areas' demand for coastal reclamation, and the Plan used the previous year. It will then submit the details to the NDRC.

In its national coastal reclamation Plan draft, the NDRC will review the SOA's decisions on the basis of national macroeconomic targets and the needs of economic and social development while applying the principles of moderately tight control, promotion of intensive use, protection of ecological systems, and balancing of sea and land development. The draft will then be included in the annual planning system for national economic and social development as per the specified procedures.

After the draft of the annual plan for national economic and social development is reviewed and adopted by the National People's Congress, the NDRC will issue an official document on the national coastal reclamation Plan indicators to the SOA and the development and reform authorities in coastal provinces (including autonomous regions and municipalities directly under the central government). On the basis of the values of the national indicators, the SOA will distribute the Plan to the ocean administrators in the coastal provinces (including autonomous regions and municipalities directly under the central government) (the Plan for some major cities is presented separately), who are not to pass on the plan to their subordinates.

To apply for an additional plan area when there is a strong case, the ocean administrators and the development and reform authorities at the provincial level would have to make a joint written application to the NDRC and SOA. Any additional plan area deemed necessary by the reviewers will be granted by adjusting the plan area allocated to other regions in the central government's annual plan for coastal reclamation. The additional plan area will be issued jointly by the NDRC and SOA. The unused plan area within a plan year will be canceled rather than carried over to the next year.

The national plan is mandatory and to be administered on the basis of verifiable records, while local plans are merely advisory. That is, any addition from the national plan is strictly controlled, and there are requirements on the proportions of functional coastal reclamation and land reclamation. Applying for an additional plan area at the local level is also tricky, but there is no mandatory requirement on how local authorities allocate funding between functional coastal reclamation and land reclamation. The general guideline is to encourage functional coastal reclamation while curbing land reclamation, with are commended proportional relationship. The length of shoreline occupied by functional coastal reclamation, the land reclaimed per unit length of shoreline, and the percentage of offshore area are all advisory.

4.2.2 *Administration of Plans for Coastal Reclamation*

The annual plans are administered differently for local and central plans. The local plans determine the annual maximum area of all the coastal reclamation projects reviewed (ratified and filed) by the authorities at or below the provincial level. The plans are only allocated to coastal provinces, autonomous regions, and municipalities directly under the central government (plans for some major cities are presented separately). After the State Council or provincial governments have approved the corresponding sea-use projects, the Plans will be marked by the ocean administrators at the same level as having been met. The central plans, meanwhile, determine the annual maximum area of all the coastal reclamation projects reviewed and ratified by the State Council and its relevant authorities. As the plans will not be allocated at the local levels, they will be marked as having been met directly by the SOA after the corresponding projects' sea-use is approved. The plans of coastal reclamation for construction purposes are mainly used for key construction projects at the national and local levels or for those promoted by national industrial policies, including projects for construction purposes and waste disposal. For coastal reclamation projects for regional sea-use planning, the plans are amortized annually on the basis of the approved sea-use on the planning horizon. Agricultural coastal reclamation refers only to projects for developing agriculture, forestry, and animal husbandry and excludes reclamation for marine culture. The plans are divided into those for construction and those for agriculture in the annual plan for coastal reclamation, and the two categories of plans must be used separately.

For construction projects that have to be reviewed or ratified, the feasibility study report and the project application submitted to the NDRC or the ratifying authority must be accompanied by the preliminary opinions issued by ocean administrators at the appropriate level. The preliminary opinions should specify the plan to be used. Before issuing the preliminary opinions on the use of the sea, ocean administrators below the provincial level (including some major cities) should first obtain the opinions of ocean administrators at the provincial level for plan allocation.

For construction projects that only need to be filed, the first step is filing with the NDRC or other relevant authorities. Then, a sea-use application for the project has to be submitted to an ocean administrator. Approval can proceed after an ocean administrator at the provincial level has issued an opinion on the allocation of the plan for coastal reclamation. The plan allocated at the local level should not exceed the total amount in the annual plan.

4.3 The Plan Management of Coastal Reclamation Making

Determining the plan involves following specified procedures. The Measures for the Management of Annual Land-Use Plan have been promulgated and implemented for many years. The plans for coastal reclamation can be established on the basis of the Measures, an approach that has been shown to be practical and in line with China's national conditions. The annual land-use plan covers the following plans:

(1) The plan for new construction land, including the total area of new construction land and the agricultural land or arable land requisitioned for new construction land.
(2) The plan for land development and consolidation, including the area of arable land compensated for by land development and land reclamation.
(3) The plan for arable land holdings.

The plan for new construction land is used separately for building urban zones and other key projects that must occupy a whole site, such as energy, transportation, water conservation, mining, or military facilities. Given the similarities between land from coastal reclamation and land for new construction land, the method of setting plans for the latter could be used again. The difference lies in the need to take into account the characteristics of the sea use when setting the plan for a coastal reclamation in order to judge whether sea use is warranted for the projects to be located in the coastal reclamation area.

4.3.1 *Procedures for Preparing the Annual Plan for Coastal Reclamation*

The annual plan is prepared using a combination of "top-down" and "bottom-up" procedures (Figure 4.2).

(1) *Submitting a proposal for the plan*: The local ocean authorities are responsible for working with the relevant authorities to propose coastal reclamation plans for the next year. These plans will be based on marine functional zoning, coastal reclamation management programs, plans for national economic and social development, actual use of the shoreline, and performance in plan administration in the base year (the last year). For land to be used in the plan year by key construction projects to be reviewed, ratified, and filed by the State Council or NDRC, if the land has to be acquired through coastal reclamation, the relevant industrial authorities have to propose a plan to the SOA for each project in the plan year immediately before the plan year in question. The plan also has to be

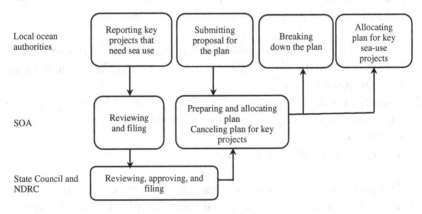

Figure 4.2   Procedures for preparing the annual plan for coastal reclamation.

copied to the ocean administrators of the province, autonomous region, or municipality under the central government in which the project is to be located.

(2) *Preparing and allocating the plan*: The SOA is required to work with the relevant authorities to prepare the annual plan for coastal reclamation in a comprehensive and balanced manner. Specifically, it should prepare the plan according to the plan for national economic and social development, national industrial policies, marine functional zoning, the program for shoreline protection and utilization, national land policies, and the plan proposal submitted by the local authorities. The plan for the new coastal reclamation projects will only be assigned to the projects to be reviewed, ratified, and filed by the authorities at or below the provincial level. For key construction projects with independent sites that require review, ratification, and filing by the State Council and NDRC, the plan for a new coastal reclamation project will not be allocated to the local levels. Instead, it will be marked as complete directly upon review of the construction projects.

(3) *Breaking down the plan*: The local authorities are responsible for revising the original plan as appropriate and preparing a draft plan for breaking down the plan. Moreover, ocean administrators at the provincial level should submit annual plans with an allocated plan to the SOA for filing.

4.3.2 *Process of Preparing the Annual Plan for Coastal Reclamation*

The preparation of the annual plan for coastal reclamation involves both research activities and administrative decision-making. On the one hand, to define the scope of the questions, set targets, design solutions, forecast results, and select the best options, the plan must be based on scientific evidence, methods, and approaches. On the other hand, as plan policies involve the adjustment and distribution of interests among numerous stakeholders, the decision-making process is bound to be rather complex, where stakeholders interact on the basis of their interests and values. As discussed in detail in what follows, the plan should be prepared on the basis of principles of comprehensive data collection, coordination of different systems, feasibility, democratic decision-making, and scientific reasoning.

(1) *Comprehensive data collection*: The preparation of an annual plan for coastal reclamation is a complex and systematic exercise. The data to be collected are quite extensive. It involves regional economic development planning, a general land-use planning, a regional transportation planning, an environmental protection planning, a marine economic development planning, as well as geological data, coastal hydrology data, marine biological data, and fishery production data (Figure 4.3). Management of coastal reclamation covers a wide range of dimensions as well as complex conflicts of interest. Therefore, preparing a reasonable and scientific annual plan for coastal reclamation first requires the comprehensive acquisition of information, with this information to be reflected in the outcomes of the plan.

(2) *Coordination with other planning*: The annual plan for coastal reclamation does not exist in isolation. It is related to the planning and policies of other administrative systems. In preparing the plan, it is necessary to underline systematic outcomes. That is, the plan must include discussions on the overall and local interests, internal and external conditions, immediate and long-term interests, and primary and secondary objectives. It should also address the interconnections, interactions, and balancing between different plans and discuss how policies at different levels are to coordinate vertically and horizontally for a better outcome, obtained by combining the policies in a way that facilitates mutual coordination and support. In particular, the plan should define the nature, role, and status of each plan as well as the administrative relationships among the plans for overall coordination and to avoid conflict.

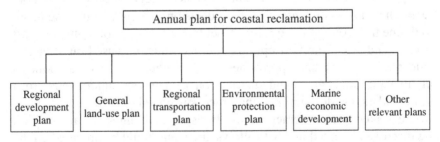

Figure 4.3   Plans related to the preparation of the annual plan for coastal reclamation.

(3) *Feasibility analysis*: The feasibility analysis in the annual plan for coastal reclamation should cover dimensions such as politics, economics, technologies, and culture, addressing a variety of changes in terms of subjective and objective conditions, including human resources, materials, financial resources, and time. By identifying robust physical conditions for the potential solutions, the exercise maximizes the feasibility and possibility of success for the implementation of the Plan. On the basis of this principle, the preparation of the annual plan for coastal reclamation relies on in-depth investigation and research into marine functional zoning and land-use planning of adjacent land areas to balance the volume of coastal reclamation and the available volume of earth and stone, thereby guiding the development and management of reclamation activities.

4.3.3 *Determining the Plan for the Coastal Reclamation*

(1) *The land-use coefficient method*: This method employs the relatively stable proportion between the variables of relevant national economic indicators and the volume of coastal reclamation to estimate the Plan for the period of the Plan.

Generally, the estimation is made on the basis of the proportion between capital investments and the area of the coastal reclamation. Using this method, the estimator should first calculate this proportion, using data from previous periods (or data for other advanced regions, controlling for differences in terms of location, topography, and geomorphy). The trend of changes in proportion should then be predicted to identify an appropriate coefficient. The total area of coastal reclamation in the plan period can be obtained by multiplying the proportion by the planned capital investment in the same period.

However, this method has several limitations. First, capital investment demands for coastal reclamation vary substantially. For example, in some regions, investments are used mostly to acquire equipment. Second, the demands change over different project stages. Third, many factors influence the scale of demands for coastal reclamation, and not all of them correlate with the scale in an exact linear manner.

(2) *Analysis of factors*: This method involves identifying relevant factors and generating an equation to calculate the Plan.

The first step is to identify the factors influencing the scale of coastal reclamation, such as capital investment, gross domestic product (GDP), population growth rate, per capita income, and other economic and social factors. The second step is to collect historical data on these influencing factors and estimate the regression equation for the indicators and the scale of coastal reclamation. The demands for coastal reclamation in the plan period can be obtained by inputting the values of the plan period into the equation.

In comparison with the land-use coefficient method, this approach is capable of producing results that are more realistic because multiple factors are taken into consideration.

(3) *Weighted moving average method*: The premise behind using this method is that the closer the reclamation data are to the plan period, the greater the influence of the data on the future demands in the reclamation plan, and this should be reflected by weighting. The farther away the reclamation data are from the reclamation plan period, the weaker the impact will be, and thus the smaller the weight. The weighted average of the investment coefficient for reclamation in previous years can be calculated as the investment coefficient for reclamation in the plan year. This coefficient is multiplied by the capital investment during the plan period to calculate the reclamation demand Plan for the plan year.

Assuming that in the last three years, the reclamation investment coefficient was d_{i-3}, d_{i-2}, and d_{i-1}, respectively, how much is the plan for coastal reclamation in the fourth year? The coefficient for year 4 is set by the weighted moving average of the coefficients of the preceding three years; with the weighting for years 1, 2, and 3 set at, for the sake of illustration, at 1, 2, and 3, the investment coefficient for year 4 can be calculated with the following equation:

$$m_i = \frac{1}{1+2+3}\left[d_{i-3} \times 1 + d_{i-2} \times 2 + d_{i-1} \times 3\right] = \frac{1}{6}\left[d_{i-3} + 2d_{i-2} + 3d_{i-1}\right], \quad (4.1)$$

where m is the investment coefficient of coastal reclamation for the plan year, d is the coefficient for the previous several years, and i denotes the year.

Similarly, the investment coefficient of reclamation in year 5 is the weighted average of the coefficient for years 2, 3, and 4, and the weight is still 1, 2, 3, and so on.

(4) *Summation of planned projects*: The sum of all the planned coastal reclamation projects and their sea-use areas for the plan period can be

defined as the scale of demands for coastal reclamation in the same period.

For accurate prediction of the sea-use scale in the plan period, this approach requires the collection of comprehensive data about the coastal reclamation projects, the renovation projects, and the coastal reclamation projects that have already been approved. Although it is highly accurate, the burden of work is relatively substantial (Yang Liu and Feng Aiping, 2011; Anning Suo *et al.*, 2012a).

4.4 System for Calculating Plans of Coastal Reclamation

The system is built on the outcomes of a project titled "Setting of Plan for Coastal Reclamation for Coastal Provinces, Municipalities Directly under the Central Government, and Autonomous Regions (Some Major Cities)." The system encapsulates the "reclamation scale prediction model based on six leading factors, such as investment and construction demands and potential in coastal reclamation resources." It has features such as forecasting of the Plans needed by coastal reclamation activities, data management, and automatic generation of reports for predicted results. Powered by geographic information system (GIS) technologies, the system can also be used to investigate or calculate the environmental carrying capacity for coastal reclamation just by navigating on a map (see Figure 4.4).

The system has been developed on the basis of Microsoft .Net Framework 3.5 and employed ArcEngine 9.3 as its GIS platform. For proper operation, the system requires the installation of Microsoft.Net Framework 3.5 and ArcGIS Desktop 9.3 or ArcEngine 9.3. With regard to hardware, CPU frequency needs to be more than 2G, memory must be more than 2G, and the available hard disk space required is 3.2G.

4.4.1 *Inquiry into and Statistics on the Carrying Capacity of Coastal Reclamation Resources*

Integrated survey data on coastal reclamation resource carrying capacity, remote sensing imagery, basic geographic information base map data, and electronic map browsing function provided by GIS can produce the features of map browsing for coastal reclamation carrying capacity (see Figure 4.5).

Figure 4.4 Interface of a module in the system for calculating plans of coastal reclamation.

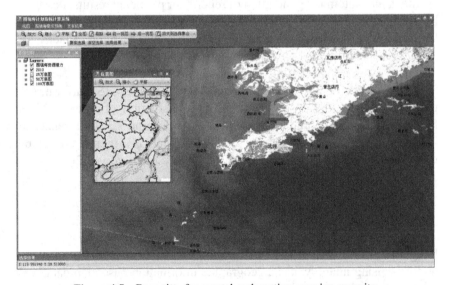

Figure 4.5 Browsing for coastal reclamation carrying capacity.

Map browsing tools:

Location map: During map browsing, the position displayed in the map browsing window can be updated in real time by using a red box in the "Location Map" window.

Toggle switch for image layers: used to control the display of map layers, such as switching on or off the remote sensing image layer.

Map inquiry tools: 围填海资源潜力 ▼ 要素选择 清空选择 选择结果 ▼

To choose the map element layer through the layer selection drop-down box on the map inquiry toolbar, with the layer selected, select the "Element Selection" tool for dragging on the map for inquiry. The "Clear Selection" button can be used to clear the selection. If the selected results window is hidden, click the "Selected Results" button to display the selected results window.

Open the data management window for coastal reclamation carrying capacity by clicking the sub-menu of "Coastal Reclamation Carrying Capacity" under the main menu of "Coastal Reclamation Demand Prediction." The data in the datasheet can be filtered by entering the required criteria in "Year," "Province/City," and "Name." For example, if 2011 is entered into "Year," all data from 2011 can be filtered out. The

ID	级别	名称	保护区	围填海资...	未来10年...	旅游区	油气资源区	渔业资源区	港口航道	泄洪排涝...	5米等深...	年份
1	省	辽宁省	152041.2	234340.3	46860.1	43957.1	0	0	29559.9	14459.6	474356.1	2011
2	省	河北省	8937.2	85809.92	17162	8162.6	44170	0	19989.1	6064	173040.6	2011
3	省	天津市	17745.3	59336.6	11867.3	5927.8	0	6190	4163.8		93363.5	2011
4	省	山东省	97463.3	116152.6	23230.6	14761.8	10228.9	211750.8	28551.7	30787.1	509796.1	2011
5	省	江苏省	61235.4	429612.3	85922.5	1111.3	0	34962.5	0	4964.4	531918.4	2011
6	省	上海市	71060.7	36591.3	7318.3	0	0	15810	8236.3	44667.5	176365.2	2011
7	省	浙江省	24576.1	258801.1	51760.2	15249	0	28338.6	0	44969.4	371934.2	2011
8	省	福建省	55658.7	179486.7	35897.3	27255.1	0	8603.8	4950	60868.8	336823.1	2011
9	省	广东省	195508.9	255543	51108.6	71713.9	0	0	2284.6	75732.8	600783.2	2011
10	省	广西自治区	103073.6	55645.9	11129.2	58523.5	0	0	4428.7	1842.1	223513.7	2011
11	省	海南省	32694.4	78457.2	15691.5	29224.6	0	0	3261.7	6350.7	149987.6	2011
12	市	大连市	7378.2	111891.4	22378.3	24953.6	0	0	11606.3	8281.2	164110.7	2011
13	市	青岛市	11432.7	41003.3	8200.7	4321.5	0	0	5699	589.6	63046	2011
14	市	宁波市	0	4289.5	957.9	1769	0	0	0	0	6058.5	2011
15	市	厦门市	6268.7	3543.4	708.7	7477	0	0	1253	14445.5	32987.6	2011
16	市	深圳市	1714.5	2200.9	440.2	464.9	0	0	0	0	4380.3	2011

围填海资源潜力:234340.3 未来10年围填海潜力:46860.1 5米等深线国内合计:474356.1 渔业资源区:0 保护区:152041.2 旅游区:43957.1 油气资源区:0 港口航道:29559.9 泄洪排涝通道:14459.6

Figure 4.6 Inquiry and statistics on coastal reclamation carrying capacity.

filter can be cleared by 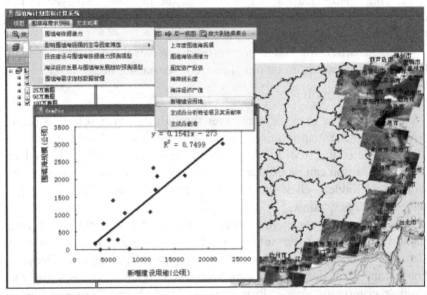 "×" in the lower-left corner. Click
the "Conditional Query" button to open the conditional query panel to use
advanced data filtering capabilities. The feature supports the combination
of multiple conditions in all fields. The selected data can be counted by

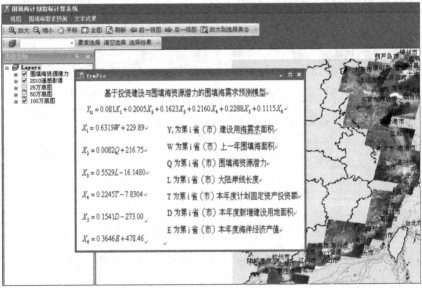

Figure 4.7 Forecasting model of coastal reclamation demand.

selecting rows in the "Row Selection Box" to the left of the datasheet, and the statistical results are displayed in the status bar (see Figure 4.6).

4.4.2 *Information on the Forecasting Model for Coastal Reclamation Demand*

This shows the results of the principal component analysis for the leading factors in the forecasting model for coastal reclamation demand, as well as the "forecasting model for the scale of coastal reclamation, based on leading indicators such as capital investment demand and potential in the resources for coastal reclamation" (see Figure 4.7).

4.4.3 *Data Management for Indicators Related to Coastal Reclamation Demand*

Open the data management window for indicators related to coastal reclamation demand by clicking the sub-menu of "Data Management for Indicators Related to Coastal Reclamation Demand" in the main menu's

Id	省	年份	上年度围...	大陆岸线...	围填海资...	海洋经济...	新增建设...	固定资产...
1	辽宁	2011	3115.73	2110	234340.29	2996.2	11218.18	12138.22
2	河北	2011	2696.02	484	85809.92	619.52	15581.73	11805.97
3	天津	2011	1401.68	153	59336.6	3079.89	6500	4532.62
4	山东	2011	1292.58	3345	116152.55	6600	13354.55	22000
5	江苏	2011	590.31	743	429612.29	2496.48	15000	19965
6	上海	2011	0	214	36591.29	5499.8	3800	7000
7	浙江	2011	2827.54	1963	258801.14	5398.25	9927.27	14000
8	福建	2011	2502.56	3752	179486.72	4502.4	8681.82	8000
9	广东	2011	119.15	4114	255542.97	7199.5	16354.55	16000
10	广西	2011	1068.05	1628	55645.88	244.2	11318.18	6000
11	海南	2011	279.8	1822	78457.23	710.58	3554.55	1200

Figure 4.8 Parameter input data for the forecasting model of coastal reclamation demand.

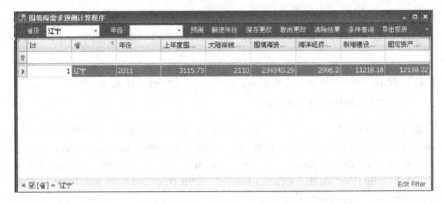

Figure 4.9 Inquiry about parameter input data for the forecasting model of coastal reclamation demand.

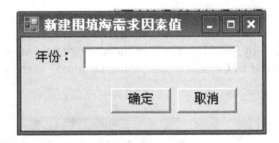

Figure 4.10 Inquiry parameter input data for the forecasting model of coastal reclamation demand.

"Coastal Reclamation Demand Prediction." The window can be used for inquiries into and management of data for indicators related to coastal reclamation demand (see Figure 4.8).

The data in the datasheet can be filtered by selecting from the "Province" and "Year" drop-down boxes. For example, selecting "Liaoning" in "Province" will filter out the data from each year for Liaoning Province. The filter can be cleared by ⟨×☑[省] = '辽宁'⟩ "×" in the lower-left corner (see Figure 4.9).

Click "Create a Year" and enter the desired year for data (see Figure 4.10). Then enter the values for each indicator for each region in the year. Click "Save Changes" to save the data after all inputs have been entered.

4.4.4 *Forecast Report of Required Plan for Coastal Reclamation*

In the data management toolbar for required plan for coastal reclamation, filter the data by "Year" and then click "Generate Report" to generate forecast reports of the demand for coastal reclamation in the specified year.

Chapter 5

Control of the Total Area
of Coastal Reclamation

5.1 Control of the Total Area of Coastal Reclamation through Marine Functional Zoning

Marine functional zoning is a type of marine spatial planning. It allocates marine spaces to different functional zones based on factors like natural resources, the natural environment, and the geographical location of a sea area and its adjacent land, with due consideration for the current usage of the sea area and the demand generated by social and economic development (Daoming Guan and a Dong, 2013). It is a tool for guiding and regulating marine development and utilization, used to realize the potential of resources and the environment and to maximize the social and economic benefits of tapping marine resources. The Law of the People's Republic of China on the Administration of Sea Areas Use designated marine functional zoning as an essential tool for marine administration, stating that "marine functional zoning is a nationwide requirement and should be followed for all sea area usage." Marine functional zoning is implemented at four administrative levels: country, province, city, and county. Country-level or national zoning involves (Xinchun Pan, 2014):

(1) assigning primary and some key secondary zones to several essential functions on a sound scientific basis;
(2) introducing critical measures for the zones' development and protection and imposing relevant restrictions on coastal reclamation;

(3) defining the significant functions of key sea areas nationwide;
(4) preparing significant support measures for zoning implementation. Province-level marine functional zoning is implemented based on national zoning. It entails:

(a) assigning appropriate zones of primary and secondary categories to several essential functions within a province's jurisdiction;
(b) developing the spatial distribution plan for the primary functional zones, introducing their development and protection measures, and imposing restrictions on coastal reclamation;
(c) functional zoning of the adjacent sea areas and defining their significant functions;
(d) preparing the significant support measures for zoning implementation.

Marine functional zoning at the city and county levels further defines in detail the primary marine functional zones based on the province-level zoning, the natural properties of the sea area, and the level of social and economic development. It outlines the agenda for zone development and protection in the short term, the sequence of the development activities, and the requirements and measures for environmental protection. It also proposes steps for implementing the zoning, specific support measures, and policy recommendations.

5.1.1 *Restrictions on Coastal Reclamation in Each of the Basic Marine Functional Zones*

The National Marine Functional Zoning (2011–2020) classifies the basic marine functional zones into eight primary and 22 secondary categories. The eight primary category zones are agricultural and fishery zones; port and shipping zones; industrial and urban construction zones; mining and energy zones; tourism, leisure, and entertainment zones; marine protection zones; special use zones; and reserved zones. The remaining part of this subsection briefly describes the restrictions on coastal reclamation in each of the primary categories.

(1) *Agricultural and fishery zones*: The zones in this category are suitable for developing agriculture and marine biological resources. Therefore, they can be used for agricultural purposes, to build fishery infrastructures like fishing ports and nurseries, for marine aquaculture/proliferation and

fishing-related production, and as conservation zones for essential fishery species. They comprise agricultural zones, fishing infrastructure zones, aquaculture zones, proliferation zones, fishing zones, and conservation zones. In these zones, coastal reclamation can only be carried out for agricultural or fishery-related production. However, even the authorized coastal reclamation activities should preferably be of moderate scale and with reasonable construction schedules. In the construction of fishing ports and ocean-going bases, the sea area should be used frugally and intensively. The spawning, feeding, and wintering grounds, as well as the migratory passages related to fishery resources, should be supervised with enhanced measures. No sluice gates, dams, or other structures that may hamper the migration of fish are permitted in these grounds or passages.

(2) *Port and shipping zones*: The zones are the sea areas with suitable resources for navigation and port development. They can be used for the construction of ports, waterways, and anchorages and are thus referred to as port, waterway, and anchorage zones, respectively. In these zones, coastal reclamation activities are permitted exclusively for infrastructure and auxiliary facilities, such as piers, harbor basins, and storage yards, with priority given to the development of major coastal ports at the national level. There are several requirements related to the construction of infrastructure and auxiliary facilities. These include enhancement of the consolidation of the shoreline resources of ports, optimization of their spatial distribution, control of their scale of construction as appropriate, assurance of intensive and efficient use of the shoreline and sea area, and maintenance of consistency with the coastal city's overall urban planning.

(3) *Industrial and urban construction zones*: The zones comprising industrial construction zones and urban construction zones are the sea areas that are suitable for the development of coastal industries and coastal towns. For coastal reclamation activities in these zones, priority should be given to construction projects listed in the national development strategies for the specific region, mainly by making a top priority the needs for sea use of the national pilot zones for comprehensive reforms, the economic and technological development zones, the high-tech industrial development zones, the circular economy demonstration zones, and the bonded port zones. Preferred industries in coastal reclamation include those encouraged by the country's industrial policies. The projects for comprehensive

utilization of seawater are also encouraged. Industrial projects that are energy, pollution, and resource intensive should be strictly controlled. Coastal reclamation activities for industrial and urban construction should be carried out frugally and intensively. Moreover, the activities must be in line with the overall planning for land use, for urban and rural development, and for estuary flood control and comprehensive consolidation. Other requirements include:

(a) controlling the area of coastal reclamation properly;
(b) optimizing the spatial distribution of the projects;
(c) improving overall efficacy of spatial resource use in a sea area;
(d) building offshore and artificial islands where possible;
(e) minimizing the impact to the marine hydrodynamic environment, tidal flat, and the seafloor topography, and
(f) preventing coastal erosion.

(4) *Mining and energy zones*: The zones are the sea areas suitable for the development of mining resources and offshore energy, for the exploration and exploitation of oil, gas, and other solid minerals, and for the development of salt farms and renewable energy. They comprise oil and gas zones, solid minerals zones, salt farm zones, and renewable energy zones. In these zones, coastal reclamation activities are mainly undertaken for the construction of salt farms. Specific requirements are maintaining a stable farm area and preventing the conversion of the farms into construction sites.

(5) *Tourism, leisure, and entertainment zones*: The zones in this category are suitable for the development of tourism attractions and for the construction of maritime cultural, sports, and recreational facilities by tapping the coastal and maritime tourism resources. They comprise scenic tourism zones and cultural, sports, and recreational zones. The latter zones are mainly located near coastal national scenic spots, national tourism resorts, national geological parks, and national forest parks or in sea areas with abundant tourism resources. In these zones, coastal reclamation activities are subject to strict control and are only permitted for the construction of tourism, leisure, and entertainment infrastructure. However, even the permitted coastal reclamation activities should preferably be of a moderate area, have an optimized spatial distribution of projects, and tap important tourism resources, such as the shoreline, bay, and islands, in an orderly manner. Non-public facilities should not be built using public tourism

resources. Other requirements include the implementation of strong protective measures for the ecological environment and protection of the coastal natural landscapes and beach resources.

(6) *Marine protection zones*: These zones, comprising marine natural protection zones and marine special protection zones, are the sea areas that are used exclusively for the protection of marine resources, the environment, and ecological systems. In these zones, coastal reclamation activities are strictly prohibited. Sea-use activities that may impact or disturb the protected areas should be significantly restricted. In sea areas that are about to be designated as marine protection zones, no construction activities are permitted.

(7) *Special use zones*: These zones are sea areas used for scientific research, teaching, and other special purposes. Specifically, the purposes include the laying of submarine pipelines, construction of roads and bridges, discharging of authorized effluents, and dumping. Marine development activities within military zones are to be restricted, and construction of other permanent structures within the areas for floor pipelines, bridges, and tunnels are to be strictly prohibited. The dumping zones are mostly used for dumping dredged materials from the construction or maintenance of large and medium-area national ports, estuaries, and waterways.

(8) *Reserved zones*: Reserved zones are sea areas for which the functions are not yet clear and for which the specific uses need to be determined through scientific demonstration. The use of the sea, such as coastal reclamation and other activities that significantly change the natural properties of the sea areas, are to be strictly restricted within these zones. Even projects that are necessary should be subject to rigorous planning and demonstration and to the due processes of hearing, public disclosure, and approval before commencement.

5.1.2 *Spatial Distribution Requirements and Other Restrictions on Coastal Reclamation in Each of the Basic Marine Functional Zones*

Under the National Marine Functional Zoning (2011–2020), the sea areas under China's jurisdiction are classified according to the sea, of which there are five: the Bohai Sea, the Yellow Sea, the East China Sea, the South China Sea, and the sea east of Taiwan. These cover 29 key sea areas. The spatial distribution of the industrial and urban construction zones that are suitable for large-scale coastal reclamation activities are discussed in detail for each of the seas as follows.

(1) *The Bohai Sea*: In the Bohai Sea areas, coastal reclamation activities are controlled to the strictest extent, especially for large-scale reclamation. The policy aims at (a) curbing the excessive consumption of sea resources due to economic growth in the Pan-Bohai region; (b) realizing the frugal and intensive use of shorelines; and (c) imposing strict control on the area of the sea area used by projects with heavy pollution, high energy consumption, elevated ecological risks, and intensive resource consumption. The industrial and urban construction zones that are suitable for large-scale coastal reclamation include:

(i)   the Pulandian Bay coastal town construction zone;
(ii) the Changxing Island port shipping and industrial construction zone;
(iii) the industrial and urban construction zone near and to the east of the estuary of the Daliaohe River;
(iv) the Tangshan Caofeidian industrial and urban construction zone;
(v)   the Tianjin Binhai New Area industry and urban construction zone;
(vi) the Cangzhou Bohai New Area industry and urban construction zone;
(vii) the Longkou Port industrial zone and construction zone.

(2) *The Yellow Sea*: In the Yellow Sea areas, the general guidelines are for rational planning of reclamation for arable land in coastal areas of Jiangsu Province, to make efficient use of the silted tidal flat resources, and to strictly restrict coastal reclamation activities in the sandy coastal areas in the north of the Shandong Peninsula. The industrial and urban construction zones that are suitable for large-scale coastal reclamation include:

(i) the industrial and urban construction zone in the south of Dalian city;
(ii) the industrial and urban construction zone in the sea area near Zhuanghe;

(iii) the Huayuankou industrial and urban construction zone;

(iv) the Dayao Bay, Xiaoyao Bay, and the industrial and urban construction zone on the tip of Dalian Bay;

(v) the industrial and urban construction zone in the southwest part of Qingdao;

(vi) the industrial and urban construction zone in the south of Rizhao;

(vii) the Lianyungang industrial and urban construction zone;

(viii) the industrial and urban construction zone between the estuaries of Guanhe and Sheyanghe;

(ix) the industrial and urban construction zone to the south of the Sheyanghe estuary.

(3) *The East China Sea*: In these sea areas, given the jagged shoreline and numerous bays and islands, the general guidelines are that moderate reclamation for arable land on tidal flats near estuaries is permitted, coastal reclamation in bays or that connects islands should be restricted, and the coastal wetland resources and the geomorphological features of the islands should be conserved. The industrial and urban construction zones that are suitable for large-scale coastal reclamation include:

(i) the industrial and urban construction zone on the sea area near Ningbo;

(ii) the industrial and urban construction zone between the Oujiang River estuary and the Zhejiang–Fujian borderline;

(iii) the Shacheng Port industrial and urban construction zone;

(iv) the Sansha Bay industrial and urban construction zone;

(v) the Luoyuan Bay industrial and urban construction zone;

(vi) the Huangqi Peninsula industrial and urban construction zone;

(vii) the Xinghua Bay industrial and urban construction zone;

(viii) the industrial and urban construction zone in Xiamen Bay and adjacent sea areas;

(ix) the industrial and urban construction zone near the Fujian–Guangdong borderline.

(4) *The South China Sea*: The South China Sea is critical to China's strategies because it has enormous marine resources, including abundant marine oil, gas, and mineral resources, coastal and island tourism resources, ocean energy resources, port and shipping resources, and unique tropical and

subtropical biological resources. It is also home to numerous essential tropical ecological systems, such as islands and coral reefs, mangroves, and seaweed beds, and so, efforts should be made to protect these marine ecological systems. In narrow estuarine areas like the Shiziyang, coastal reclamation for land should be controlled strictly. The industrial and urban construction zones that are suitable for large-scale coastal reclamation include:

   (i) the industrial and urban construction zone between the Nan'ao and Guang'ao Bays;
  (ii) the industrial and urban construction zone from Haimen Bay to Shequan Port;
 (iii) the Lingdingyang industrial and urban construction zone;
 (iv) the Zhenhai Bay industrial and urban construction zone;
  (v) the Hailing Bay industrial and urban construction zone;
 (vi) the Zhanjiang Port industrial and urban construction zone;
(vii) the Tieshan Port industrial and urban construction zone;
(viii) the Lianzhou Bay industrial and urban construction zone;
 (ix) the Fangcheng Port industrial and urban construction zone.

5.1.3 *Targets for Controlling the Total Area of Coastal Reclamation Specified in the Marine Functional Zoning*

The National Marine Functional Zoning (2011–2020), approved by the State Council in 2012, imposed several requirements on coastal reclamation, including:

   (i) control of the area of coastal reclamation as appropriate;
  (ii) strict implementation of the annual plan regime for coastal reclamation;
 (iii) prevention of excessive coastal reclamation;
 (iv) maintenance of the area of coastal reclamation in line with macroeconomic targets and the carrying capacity of the marine ecological environment.

However, the zoning did not set any specific targets for the total area of coastal reclamation. Subsequently, the marine function zonings of the 11 provincial administrative regions along the coast, as approved by the

Table 5.1 Provincial targets for controlling the total area of coastal reclamation based on the marine functional zoning.

Provincial administrative regions	Total area (hm²)	Provincial administrative regions	Total area (hm²)
Liaoning	25,300	Hebei	14,950
Tianjin	9,200	Shandong	34,500
Jiangsu	26,450	Shanghai	2,300
Zhejiang	50,600	Fujian	33,350
Guangdong	23,000	Guangxi	16,100
Hainan	11,150		

State Council, all put forward 11 specific targets to be achieved by 2020 (Table 5.1). The sum of the provincial targets is 246,900 hm², which also represents the national total by 2020. In terms of provincial figures, Zhejiang Province had the highest target of acquiring land through coastal reclamation for construction projects at 50,600 hm², followed by Shandong and Fujian, which had targets of 34,500 hm², and 33,350 hm², respectively. For Jiangsu, Liaoning, and Guangdong, the targets were 26,450 hm², 25,300 hm², and 23,000 hm², respectively. Other provincial administrative regions had targets within 20,000 hm², while Tianjin and Shanghai had targets of only 9,200 hm² and 2,300 hm², respectively.

5.2 Control of the Total Area of Coastal Reclamation Based on Cost-Benefit Analyses

In China, the huge profit margin between the gains from coastal reclamation and its costs is the primary force that drives the continuous large-scale coastal reclamation activities. While the market benchmark price determines the gains for the land from coastal reclamation, the costs are dependent on the underwater topography of the sea area where the reclamation takes place, labor costs, and other factors. This profit margin can only be maintained when the gains far exceed the costs. Therefore, in this section, we will discuss a method for controlling the total area of coastal reclamation based on cost-benefit analyses.

5.2.1 *Estimation of the Suitable Depth of the Sea Area for Coastal Reclamation*

The underwater topography in coastal waters is an important factor that influences the difficulty and cost of reclamation. Generally, if the water depth near the shore is shallow, the bottom slope is gradual, and the waves are relatively small, construction will be easier. Moreover, because a unit volume of earthworks can be used to create a larger area of land, the construction costs will also be lower. By contrast, when there is complex underwater terrain, steep slopes, rapid currents, and large waves, the construction of outer revetment work will be complicated. More importantly, as the volume of earthworks required to fill the same sea area increases substantially, the cost of reclamation will rise sharply. Thus, the underwater topography in coastal waters is an essential factor that influences the work of coastal reclamation.

Setting the depth of coastal waters as L in meters, then, for 1,000 m of the offshore sea zone, the area of reclamation is $1,000\frac{L}{tg\alpha}$ and the sectional area is $\frac{L^2}{2tg\alpha}$. The volume of the whole zone (or the volume of the earthworks required for coastal reclamation) V can be calculated as the product of the sectional area S and the reclamation length, that is, $V = \frac{L^2}{2tg\alpha} \times 1,000$.

According to an investigation of several reclamation projects in the coastal zones of Liaoning, Hebei, and Shandong, the average cost of earthworks is 140 Yuan per cubic meter. Therefore, the total cost for the reclamation volume $V = \frac{L^2}{2tg\alpha} \times 1,000$ is $140\ V$, or $\frac{L^2}{2tg\alpha} \times 140,000$ Yuan, which can be simplified as $\frac{70,000\ L^2}{tg\alpha}$.

The coastal reclamation projects are only profitable when their costs are smaller than the benchmark price of land gained from coastal reclamation. Otherwise, large-scale reclamation activities will not be sustainable. According to the above investigation, the benchmark price in coastal zones is 350 Yuan per square meter (Minghui Zhang *et al.*, 2013). Therefore, the following equation can express the conditions.

$$\frac{70,000\ L^2}{tg\alpha} \leq \frac{1000\ L \times 350}{tg\alpha} \tag{5.1}$$

$$L \leq 5.$$

In other words, a depth of 5.0 m is the maximum suitable depth for reclamation projects. Only those projects with a depth of fewer than 5.0 m are profitable, with a cost less than the benchmark price of 350.00 Yuan per square meter. Otherwise, when costs are higher than the market benchmark price, large-scale reclamation projects will not be appropriate from the perspective of economic benefits (Xia Lin *et al.*, 2015).

5.2.2 *An Approach for Evaluating the Carrying Capacity of Spatial Resources*

The industrial and urban construction zones in marine functional zoning are mostly located in the sea areas near large or medium cities and essential ports. They are mainly used for constructing coastal industrial bases, industrial parks, and coastal towns. Therefore, to evaluate the carrying capacity for coastal reclamation, in this book, we mostly consider industrial and urban construction zones. Other basic marine functional zones, such as port and shipping functional zones, agricultural and fishery zones, and tourism, leisure, and entertainment zones, are given less weightage because they make up a smaller part of coastal reclamation.

As a proxy, industrial and urban construction zones with suitable costs, that is, within the areas between the natural coastline and the −5 m isobath, are treated as the distribution zones of the carrying capacity for coastal reclamation (Shuxi Liu, and Sun Shuyan, 2013).

The zones with suitable costs can be obtained by overlaying the vector data of marine functional zoning for 11 coastal provincial administrative regions onto the −5 m isobath data from the 1:50,000 terrain data. The remaining areas, after deducting the areas for passages of flood flows, tidal passages, and other factors that render them unfit for coastal reclamation, comprise the distribution zones of the carrying capacity.

The area sum of the distribution zones for the 11 regions is treated as the carrying capacity of the next 50 years. As shown in Table 5.2, the sum is divided into the total area to be controlled in the next 5, 10, and 20 years.

Of the national total of 1,789,776.90 hm², the carrying capacity for coastal reclamation allocated to the next 10 years is 357,955.60 hm². Jiangsu has the largest capacity, with an area of 85,922.50 hm², accounting for 24.0% of the national total to be controlled. It is followed by

Table 5.2 The carrying capacity for coastal reclamation and the total area to be controlled for each coastal provincial administrative region based on cost–benefit analyses (unit: hm²).

Region	−5.0 m isobath total area	Carrying capacity for coastal reclamation	Total area to be controlled (next 20 years)	Total area to be controlled (next 10 years)	Total area to be controlled (next 5 years)
Liaoning	474,358.10	234,340.30	93,736.20	46,868.10	23,434.05
Dalian	164,110.70	111,891.40	44,756.60	22,378.30	11,189.15
Hebei	173,040.60	85,809.92	34,324.00	17,162.00	8,581.00
Tianjin	93,363.50	59,336.60	23,734.60	11,867.30	5,933.65
Shandong	509,796.10	116,152.60	46,461.20	23,230.60	11,615.30
Qingdao	63,046.00	41,003.30	16,401.40	8,200.70	4,100.35
Jiangsu	531,918.40	429,612.30	171,845.00	85,922.50	42,961.25
Shanghai	176,365.20	36,591.30	14,636.60	7,318.30	3,659.15
Zhejiang	371,934.20	258,801.10	103,520.40	51,760.20	25,880.10
Ningbo	6,058.50	4,289.50	1,715.80	857.90	428.95
Fujian	336,823.10	179,486.70	71,794.60	35,897.30	17,948.65
Xiamen	32,987.60	3,543.40	1,417.40	708.70	354.35
Guangdong	600,783.20	255,543.00	102,217.20	51,108.60	25,554.30
Shenzhen	4,380.30	2,200.90	880.40	440.20	220.10
Guangxi	223,513.70	55,645.90	22,258.40	11,129.20	5,564.60
Hainan	149,987.60	78,457.20	31,383.00	15,691.50	7,845.75
Total	3,912,466.80	1,789,776.90	715,910.80	357,955.60	178,977.70

Zhejiang, which has an area of 51,760.20 hm² and accounts for 14.46% of the national total. Guangdong ranks third, with an area of 51,108.60 hm², accounting for 14.28% of the national total. Liaoning (46,868.10 hm²), Fujian (35,897.30 hm²), and Shandong (23,230.60 hm²) follow.

5.3 Control of the Total Area of Coastal Reclamation Based on Demand Forecasting

Social and economic development in coastal regions is the fundamental driving force behind the demand for coastal reclamation. To control the total area of coastal reclamation, it is critical to distinguish between the demand from social and economic development and the demand from pure speculation, to identify the different driving forces behind coastal reclamation activities, and to forecast the first type of demand on a scientific basis. In this section, we will develop a method for forecasting coastal reclamation demand from the perspective of social and economic demand, as well as the carrying capacity of the resources. The method will be applied to forecast real demand, which will serve as the basis for controlling the area of coastal reclamation.

5.3.1 *Screening of Leading Factors That Affect Coastal Reclamation Demand*

The factors that affect coastal reclamation demand can be categorized under various headings, including social factors, economic factors, resource conditions, and policy factors. As the policy factor is highly volatile and hard to quantify, social, economic, and resource factors are used to forecast the demands for coastal reclamation in China. The preliminary selection of the factors is based on this book's previous conclusion about the factors affecting coastal reclamation demand. The list of factors is expanded following a brainstorming session of experts from ocean administration and marine scientific research institutions. Table 5.3 summarizes the factors.

As can be seen in Table 5.4, a correlation analysis of the factors listed in Table 5.3 finds that coastal reclamation is significantly correlated to the area of the previous year's coastal reclamation, the total regional population, regional GDP, investments in fixed assets, the carrying capacity for coastal reclamation, and shoreline length; correlation with other factors is insignificant. Consequently, these six factors are considered as the main factors affecting the extent of demand for coastal reclamation. Table 5.4, which is a correlation matrix for those factors, shows that:

(1) the area of coastal reclamation correlates most closely with the carrying capacity, with a correlation coefficient of 0.837 and a significance level of 0.001%;
(2) the correlation with the previous year's area of coastal reclamation ranks second, with a correlation coefficient of 0.819 and a significance level of 0.001%;
(3) the correlation with shoreline length ranks third, with a correlation coefficient of 0.797 and a significance level of 0.001%;

Table 5.3 Factors affecting coastal reclamation with relevant descriptions.

Factor	Description	Definition	Data source
Current status of coastal reclamation	Area of previous year's coastal reclamation	Reflecting the development trend and technical level of coastal reclamation	Bulletin on the administration of the use of sea areas
	Benefits from using the reclaimed land	Reflecting the economic benefits brought by the reclaimed land	Bulletin on the administration of the use of sea areas and data collected in the survey and consultation processes
	Intensity of investment in coastal reclamation per unit area	Reflecting the investment intensity in developing the reclaimed land	Sea-area use demonstration report and relevant data
Condition of resources	Shoreline length	Reflecting the potential of reclamation to a certain extent	The results of shoreline restoration and measurement as approved by governments at the appropriate levels
	Carrying capacity for coastal reclamation	Reflecting the carrying capacity for coastal reclamation to a certain extent (after subtracting the area of reclaimed land registered after the enactment of the Sea Area Law)	Forecast Report on the National Demands for Coastal Reclamation in the Next 10 Years (SOA, 2011)
Demand from social and economic development	Marine economic output per unit length of shoreline	Reflecting the economic benefits generated from using a unit length of shoreline	Yearbook of Marine Economic Statistics
	Investments in fixed assets	Reflecting the tightness of macroeconomic regulation on regional economic development	Statistical yearbook of provinces/ municipalities

GDP	Reflecting the degree of regional economic development	Statistical yearbook of provinces/ municipalities
Urbanization rate	Reflecting the land demands for residential and infrastructural purposes due to increase in non-agricultural population	Statistical yearbook of provinces/ municipalities
Rate of economic growth	Reflecting indirectly the land demands that are in line with the degree of regional economic development	Statistical Bulletin of National Economic and Social Development; Statistical yearbook of Chinese Cities and Provinces; Statistical yearbook of provinces/municipalities
Yield per unit area of land	Reflecting the difference in output potential and benefits from land use of the reclaimed land in different regions	Statistical yearbooks of governments and websites of land bureaus at different levels
The proportion of the regional marine economy in GDP	Reflecting the degree of marine economic development	Yearbook of Marine Economic Statistics
Area of the population	Reflecting the demands for industrial, commercial, and infrastructural land due to regional population agglomeration	Statistical yearbook of provinces/ municipalities

Table 5.4   Correlation matrix of the leading factors affecting coastal reclamation.

	Area of coastal reclamation	Population	Area of previous year's coastal reclamation	Shoreline length	Investment in fixed assets	GDP	Carrying capacity for coastal reclamation
Area of coastal reclamation	1	0.734 $P = 0.003$	0.819 $P = 0.001$	0.797 $P = 0.001$	0.762 $P = 0.002$	0.648 $P = 0.012$	0.837 $P = 0.001$
Area of previous year's coastal reclamation		1	0.760 $P = 0.001$	0.815 $P = 0.000$	0.922 $P = 0.000$	0.918 $P = 0.000$	0.700 $P = 0.005$
Carrying capacity for coastal reclamation			1	0.837 $P = 0.000$	0.846 $P = 0.000$	0.676 $P = 0.006$	0.737 $P = 0.003$
Marine economic output				1	0.906 $P = 0.000$	0.738 $P = 0.001$	0.876 $P = 0.000$
Shoreline length					1	0.906 $P = 0.000$	0.788 $P = 0.001$
Investment in fixed assets						1	0.735 $P = 0.003$
Area of new construction sites							1

(4) the correlation with investment in fixed assets ranks fourth, with a correlation coefficient of 0.762 and a significance level of 0.002%;

(5) the correlation with population area ranks fifth, with a correlation coefficient of 0.734 and a significance level of 0.003%;

(6) the correlation with GDP ranks sixth, with a correlation coefficient of 0.648 and a significance level of 0.012%.

5.3.2 *Constructing the Model to Forecast Demand for Coastal Reclamation*

A principal component analysis (PCA) is performed to determine the loadings of the leading factors that affect the demand for coastal

Table 5.5   PCA square roots of corresponding eigenvalues and their contribution rates.

Principal component	Eigenvalue's roots	Contribution rate of the root (%)	Cumulative contribution rate (%)
1	4.490	74.835	74.835
2	0.684	11.403	86.238
3	0.415	6.909	93.147
4	0.305	5.077	98.224

reclamation. The loadings for the six leading factors are then used to calculate the weights applied to the factors (Jie Huang *et al.*, 2016b). As shown by the PCA results in Table 5.5, the biggest three square roots of the corresponding eigenvalues are 4.490, 0.684, and 0.415. Their cumulative contribution rate reaches 74.835%, 86.238%, and 93.147%, respectively, indicating that the first principal component accounts for 74.835% of the information in the raw data; the first and second principal components combined account for 86.238% of the information, and a combination of the first three principal components captures 93.147% of the information. Therefore, the first two principal components are selected for further calculation. (It is generally accepted that sufficient information can be retained when the cumulative contribution rate of principal components reaches 85%.)

As shown in Table 5.6, which presents the calculated loadings of the leading factors on each principal component, population area, investment in fixed assets, and GDP have higher loadings on the first principal component, indicating that the first principal component mainly represents the impact of social and economic development on the demand for coastal reclamation. By contrast, shoreline length, area of the previous year's coastal reclamation, and carrying capacity for coastal reclamation have higher loadings on the second principal component, indicating that the second one mainly represents the impact of the conditions of the resources on the demand for coastal reclamation.

The loadings can be used to calculate the weights to be applied to the factors. Given these weights, the forecasting model can be constructed as follows:

$$Y_i = 0.315F_{i1} + 0.685F_{i2}, \qquad (5.2)$$

Table 5.6   Loadings of the principal components.

Leading factor	First principal component	Second principal component
Population area	0.939	−0.151
Shoreline length	0.375	0.784
Investment in fixed assets	0.941	−0.238
GDP	0.927	−0.089
Area of previous year's coastal reclamation	0.454	0.895
Carrying capacity for coastal reclamation	0.624	0.921

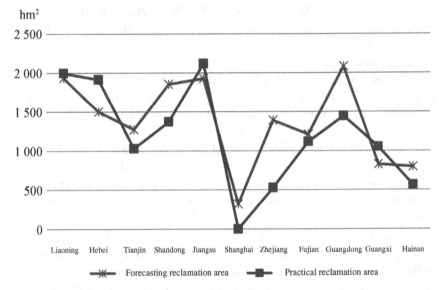

Figure 5.1   Comparison of forecast and actual area of coastal reclamation.

where

$$F_{i1} = 0.47X_{i1} + 0.016X_{i2} + 0.332X_{i3} + 0.298X_{i4} + 0.091X_{i5} + 0.176X_{i6} \text{ and}$$

$$F_{i2} = -0.187X_{i1} + 0.516X_{i2} - 0.325X_{i3} - 0.089X_{i4} + 0.613X_{i5} + 0.792X_{i6},$$

where X_{i1} is the population area of the province (municipality) i, X_{i2} denotes the shoreline length of the province (municipality) i, X_{i3} denotes investment in fixed assets of the province (municipality) i, X_{i4} denotes the GDP of the province (municipality) i, X_{i5} denotes the area of the previous year's coastal reclamation in the province (municipality) i, and X_{i6} denotes the carrying capacity for coastal reclamation of the province (municipality) i.

Using the actual figures for the year 2011, we can use the above regression model to calculate the area of coastal reclamation demand for the coastal provinces/municipalities for that year. Figure 5.1 compares the forecast values and actual values. The figure shows that the forecast and actual values were close, except for large deviations for some locations. Most of the deviations were small and within a range of 10%.

5.3.3 *Forecasting the Demand for Coastal Reclamation*

The development data series for the six factors affecting coastal reclamation in the next 10 years are established on the basis of current resource status, social and economic development trends, and the planning of coastal provinces and municipalities. The area of the previous year's coastal reclamation is the forecast value for the year. The shoreline length remains the same. The value of the carrying capacity for coastal reclamation is set by subtracting the area of previous coastal reclamation activities before the forecasting year. The marine economic output is the yearly cumulative added value in relation to the figure in 2010. The investments in fixed assets are calculated by multiplying the GDP growth rate of each region with its base value of an investment in fixed assets in 2010. The area for new construction sites is estimated for each year on the basis of the area of these sites in the 2010–2020 Ministry of Land and Resources' planning for each of the provinces/municipalities. Table 5.7 summarizes the total area of coastal reclamation to be controlled nationwide and for each of the provincial administrative regions in the next 5 and 10 years by inputting the above 2010–2020 data series for the leading factors. Over the next five years, the area of coastal reclamation to be controlled nationwide is 177,756.40 hm². Shandong ranks first, with an area of 26,091.92 hm², followed by Guangdong (23,592.99 hm²), Zhejiang (20,497.63 hm²), Jiangsu (17,613.78 hm²), and Liaoning (17,083.19 hm²). The five provinces have a large area of coastal reclamation to be controlled, but the annual average of the area is within 6,000 hm². Over the next 10 years, the area of coastal reclamation to be controlled nationwide is 386,436.30 hm². Shandong ranks

Table 5.7 Total area of coastal reclamation to be controlled based on demand forecasting.

Region	Total area to be controlled in the next 5 years (hm^2)	Total area to be controlled in the next 10 years (hm^2)
Liaoning	17,083.19	40,630.70
Hebei	10,680.72	25,420.34
Tianjin	13,180.23	25,582.45
Shandong	26,091.92	56,467.04
Jiangsu	17,613.78	40,867.64
Shanghai	15,714.45	31,192.94
Zhejiang	20,479.63	44,716.26
Fujian	18,771.66	39,862.85
Guangdong	23,592.99	49,490.17
Guangxi	7,746.75	17,498.98
Hainan	6,801.03	14,706.88
Whole of China	177,756.35	386,436.25

first, with an area of 56,467.04 hm^2, followed by Guangdong (49,490.17 hm^2), Zhejiang (44,716.26 hm^2), Jiangsu (40,867.64 hm^2), Liaoning (40,630.70 hm^2), Fujian (39,862.85 hm^2), and Shanghai (31,192.94 hm^2). These seven provinces/municipalities have a large area of coastal reclamation to be controlled in the next 10 years.

Chapter 6

Promotion of the Intensive Use of Reclaimed Land

6.1 Promoting Intensive Use through Land Reclamation Indicators

Land formed by coastal reclamation has the same functions and uses as other types of land. Therefore, indicators for promoting the intensive use of other types of land may also be employed for reclaimed land. Intensive land use can be defined as the inputting of more capital and labor into a specific area of land while employing advanced technologies and management approaches for higher output and revenue. As the inputs include capital, labor, and technologies, intensive land use can be classified as capital-intensive, labor-intensive, and technology-intensive. To measure intensity, the indicators include investment intensity, output per unit area, and land-use standards. Although it may be possible to develop reclaimed land in the same way as other types of land, the set of indicators need to be modified to take into account the fact that the land has been formed by coastal reclamation (Shuxian Sun, 2004). Many coastal reclamation projects are built along the shoreline. The reclaimed land is used to develop coastal industries, port industries, coastal towns, and coastal tourism areas, where a shoreline and a port are necessary features. How the shoreline used is essential for promoting the intensive use of reclaimed land. Therefore, building on the set of indicators measuring the intensity of land use, this section develops a system of indicators for promoting the intensive use of reclaimed land by taking into account the characteristics of development projects on reclaimed land. The indicators, namely, the investment intensity indicator, shoreline indicators, and indicators related to land-use standards, will be discussed in detail in the following subsections.

6.1.1 *Investment Intensity Indicator*

In China, technical measures, such as marine functional zoning and sea-use demonstration, can be taken to investigate whether a specific sea area is suitable for reclamation. However, they cannot be employed to determine the appropriate size of a sea-use project. Due to the lack of necessary assessment frameworks and parameters, it is impossible to define the size of reclamation activities for a project. In 2012, to promote intensive and frugal use of sea-area resources, the SOA's Department of Sea Area Management launched a research project titled "Indicators for Controlling Sea Use for Industrial Purposes." Through surveys and research, the Department set criteria for major sea-use industries in terms of investment intensity in relation to the area of sea use. In this subsection, the following model for investment intensity in coastal reclamation in relation to the area of sea use is presented based on the previously mentioned research:

$$JY_i = \frac{t_{ij}}{a_{ij} \times AT_{j0}},$$

(6.1)

where JY_i is the indicator for controlling the area of coastal reclamation for project i, t_{ij} denotes the total investment of project i in the industry j in 10,000 Yuan, a_{ij} is the area of coastal reclamation of project i in industry j in hectares, and AT_{j0} is the criterion of investment intensity in relation to the area of sea-use for industry j. Table 6.1 shows the criteria for investment intensity in relation to the area of sea use for major industries.

Table 6.1   Criteria for investment intensity in relation to the area of sea use for major industries.

Sea-use industries	Port	Shipbuilding	Electric power	Petrochemical	Other industries
Criteria for investment intensity in relation to the area of sea use (10,000 Yuan/Hectare)	2,238.64	4,903.33	12,195.12	9,025.27	3,022.98

Table 6.2 Criteria for investment intensity in relation to the length of shoreline used for major industries.

Sea-use industries	Port	Shipbuilding	Electric power	Petrochemical	Other industries
Criteria for investment intensity in relation to the length of shoreline used (10,000 Yuan/km)	83,333.33	90,909.09	500,000.00	333,333.33	20,000.00

In addition, to reflect the intensity of shoreline use of a specific coastal reclamation project, the following model of investment intensity of coastal reclamation in relation to the length of shoreline used is presented:

$$CY_i = \frac{t_{ij}}{l_{ij} \times CT_{j0}},$$

where CY_i is the indicator for controlling the length of shoreline for project i, t_{ij}, denotes the total investment of project i in industry j in 10,000 Yuan, l_{ij} denotes the length of shoreline in kilometers occupied by project i in industry j, and CT_{j0} denotes the criterion of investment intensity in relation to the length of shoreline used for industry j. Table 6.2 shows the criteria for investment intensity in relation to the length of shoreline used for major industries.

6.1.2 *Shoreline Indicators*

The natural coastline formed by the long-term interaction of sea and land serves a range of ecological functions with its stable topography and invaluable resources. Once the natural coastline is destroyed and occupied, it is challenging to restore and rebuild it. Therefore, in coastal reclamation, appropriate measures should be taken to avoid or minimize the use of the natural shoreline. In particular, forming a straight shoreline instead of the original curved ones in coastal reclamation should be guarded against, given the substantial damage, it would inflict on the natural shoreline. The coastline is also critical to the development of coastal industries, which can be classified into functional and non-functional sea-use industries. Functional sea use refers to the development of a sea area for functional purposes on the basis of the shoreline. Sea use for port construction and development of the shipbuilding industry is functional. In such cases, the ratio of the created shoreline length to the length of the original shoreline occupied, or the index of shoreline gain or loss, represents the intensity of shoreline use. Please refer to Section 3.1 for the index's calculation model and for the values assigned to the results at different grades.

Non-functional sea use refers to coastal reclamation for land that is mostly used to solve the issue of land resource shortages. It often does not need to use the sea area and shoreline. Therefore, for this type of sea use, the length of the shoreline occupied should be minimal. The use of the sea by electric power, petrochemical, and other industries is non-functional. In such cases, the area of reclaimed land per unit length of shoreline, or the index for the intensity of coastal reclamation, can be used to reflect the intensity in shoreline use. Please refer to Section 3.1 for the index's calculation model and for the values assigned to the results at different grades.

For many coastal cities and ports, the space provided by the sea is indispensable to their development. Thus, the occupation of the shoreline would affect the available sea field for the development of coastal towns and industries. Moreover, a coastal development setback zone is necessary to provide sufficient public space for activities, such as enjoyment of the waterfront, fishing, and viewing of sea landscape. Two indicators—the coastal development setback distance and setback proportion—can be used to measure the setback. The coastal development setback distance refers to the landward distance between the development site and the shoreline. Setback proportion refers to the proportion of the total length of the regional shoreline that has setback zones. For the planning and design of coastal tourism areas, the setback distance between buildings and the shoreline is generally required to be more than 30 m. In some regions, the required distance is more than 50 m. Sanya city in Hainan requires that the setback distance for buildings in Sanya Bay, Dadonghai, Xiaodonghai, Luhuitou, and Haipo be more than 80 m from the shoreline. For Yalong Bay and other special sections, the distance should be more than 100 m. According to some experts, when developing coastal industrial zones, a setback distance of more than 30 m and a proportion of no less than 20% are appropriate; when developing coastal towns, a setback distance of more than 50 m and a proportion of no less than 30% are suitable.

6.1.3 Indicators Related to Land-Use Standards

In most cases, the land formed by coastal reclamation will be developed directly. Consequently, the size of coastal reclamation can be controlled through the standards that promote intensive land use. In recent years, government authorities have introduced several standards, rules, and policies to promote intensive and frugal land use in land planning. Table 6.3 shows the composition of planned construction land as stipulated in the "Classification of Urban Land Uses and Planned Construction Land-Use Standards." The per capita urban construction land target of newly built cities should be 85.10–105.00 m^2/person, of which the per capita residential land area should be 23.00–38.00 m^2/person, the per capita land area for public administration and public service facilities should not be less than 5.50 m^2/person, and the per capita land area for roads and traffic facilities should not be less than 12.00 m^2/person. The per capita vegetation land area should not be less than 10.00 m^2/person.

In 2008, the Ministry of Land and Resources issued the "Construction Land Criteria for Industrial Projects," which established the criteria for industrial projects in terms of investment intensity, construction plot ratio, building coefficient, land area for administrative offices and living service facilities, and ratio of land for vegetation. To control the size of industrial zones built in coastal areas or near ports, criteria can be used that include plot ratio, building coefficient, land area for administrative offices and living service facilities, and the ratio of land for vegetation. Other requirements include (1) a building coefficient for industrial projects of no less than 30%, (2) a land area for administrative offices and living service facilities for industrial projects of no more than 7% of the total land area used by the projects, (3) a ban within the land used by industrial projects

Table 6.3 Composition of planned construction land.

Category	Proportion of planned construction land (%)
Residential land	25.00–40.00
Land for public administration and public service facilities	5.00–8.00
Industrial land	15.00–30.00
Land for roads and transportation facilities	12.00–30.00
Vegetation and square land	10.00–15.00

on non-productive supporting facilities, such as residential complexes, buildings exclusively for experts, hotels, guest houses, and training centers, and (4) in general, no vegetation land within an industrial enterprise. However, if a certain proportion of vegetation land is needed due to special requirements, such as a specific production technology, vegetation land can be included, although the ratio should not exceed 20%. The criteria in terms of the plot ratio for coastal industrial buildings are shown in Table 6.4.

Table 6.4   Criteria in terms of plot ratio for coastal industrial buildings.

Industrial classification		
Code	Description	Plot ratio
13	Staple and non-staple food processing	≥1.00
24	Manufacture of cultural, educational, and sports goods	≥1.00
25	Petroleum processing, coking, and nuclear fuel and its processing	≥0.50
26	Manufacture of chemical raw materials and products	≥0.60
27	Manufacture of pharmaceuticals	≥0.70
28	Manufacture of chemical fibers	≥0.80
29	Rubber manufacture	≥0.80
30	Plastics manufacture	≥1.00
31	Nonmetallic mineral products	≥0.70
32	Ferrous metal smelting and calendering	≥0.60
33	Nonferrous metal smelting and calendering	≥0.60
34	Metal products	≥0.70
35	Manufacture of general equipment	≥0.70
36	Manufacture of special equipment	≥0.70
37	Manufacture of transportation equipment	≥0.70
39	Manufacture of electrical machinery and equipment	≥0.70
40	Manufacture of communications equipment, computers, and other electronic equipment	≥1.00
41	Manufacture of instruments and culture and office machinery	≥1.00
42	Manufacture of art and craft products	≥1.00
43	Recycling and processing of discarded materials and waste	≥1.00

6.2 Promoting Intensive Use by Optimizing the Layout of Coastal Reclamation Projects

The spatial layout of coastal reclamation refers to the distribution of patterns and functions of coastal reclamation projects in the sea-area space. The outstanding design of layout and distribution of functions may not only minimize the impact of reclamation on the marine ecological environment but can also effectively enhance the value of coastal resources from coastal reclamation and improve the general intensive use of the resources in the reclamation area. The layout designs of coastal reclamation projects in China have to comply with a number of guidelines, including a shift from layout along the shoreline to artificial islands and multiple jetties and from a large block to a combination of multiple smaller blocks. In other words, the layout should be designed as much as possible using offshore features, multiple blocks, and a curved shoreline.

To optimize the layout and improve intensive use, this section provides several indicators to assess the layout design of coastal reclamation projects. The indicators are selected on the basis of extensive research on layout designs worldwide. They cover dimensions such as the sea area used, geographical location, changes to the shoreline length, waterfront shoreline created, protection of the natural shoreline, water space reserved, and passages for marine processes. They are also selected by adhering to the following principles.

(1) *Protection of the natural shoreline*: The natural shoreline serves a range of ecological functions with its stable environment and invaluable resources. Once the natural coastline is destroyed, it is challenging to restore and rebuild it. Therefore, in the construction of coastal reclamation projects, to conserve shoreline resources and ecological functions, adequate measures should be adopted to protect the natural shoreline, use of which should be avoided or minimized as possible.

(2) *Extension of the artificial shoreline*: The value of reclaimed land mainly depends on the area of newly formed land and the length of the added artificial shoreline. The longer the artificial shoreline, the greater the value of the newly formed land in terms of waterfront resources. Therefore, in the layout design of coastal reclamation projects, the artificial shoreline should be as jagged as possible to extend the length of the

artificial shoreline, thereby increasing the value of the newly formed land.

(3) *Improvement of the waterfront landscape*: A reclamation project will inevitably change the natural landscape of the original shoreline. Therefore, the development of the land from coastal reclamation should pay due attention to landscape construction. Generally, a landscape area of a certain width must be reserved landward from the artificial shoreline for the necessary vegetation and beautification. In addition, the appropriate environment and amenities must be provided so that people can enjoy the waterfront.

(4) *Intensive and frugal use of the sea*: In coastal reclamation projects, adequate measures should be adopted to protect the limited natural shoreline, the use of which should be intensive and frugal. Projects should be concentrated in specific shoreline sections because dispersed projects would occupy or damage the shoreline extensively.

(5) *Protection of the marine ecological environment*: The impact of coastal reclamation projects on the marine environment should be minimized, and the original sea area should be preserved as much as possible, particularly essential tidal flow and ecological passages. They are critical to hydrodynamic processes, the migration of marine organisms, and the maintenance of the marine ecological environment.

This section demonstrates the application of the above principles for the intensive use of sea resources and the maintenance of marine ecological functions. It applies separate assessment indicators, criteria, and models for layout design in the form of artificial islands, features along the shoreline and projecting out to the sea, and features composed of multiple blocks. As discussed in detail in *Assessing Methodologies for Coastal Reclamation* (Yonghai Yu and Suo Anning, 2013a), these indicators, criteria, and models form a technical library for assessing and optimizing the layout designs of coastal reclamation projects.

The first step for assessing a project design is to judge whether the project can be classified as an artificial island, a feature along the shoreline and projecting out to sea, or a feature that is composed of multiple blocks. On the basis of the above judgment, in the second step,

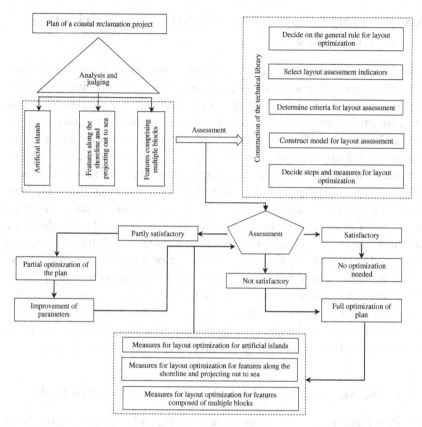

Figure 6.1 Steps for optimizing the layout of coastal reclamation projects.

appropriate indicators are selected and calculated by using parameters in the project planning. Then, the overall layout envisaged by the project planning is assessed by using a model that incorporates the grades from Step 2's results. The planning is treated differently according to the assessment of the indicators. For planning with good grades, no optimization is needed for the parameters in the planning. For planning with fairly good indicators, the parameters that need to be optimized will be identified and rectified, with specific measures for optimization. For planning with unsatisfactory indicators, the planning needs to be re-prepared by the unit responsible for its preparation. After preparing the planning, the above steps need to be repeated until the indicators can be deemed satisfactory. Figure 6.1 summarizes these steps.

6.3 Promoting Intensive Use through the Principle of User Pays

China has an emerging market for sea-use rights as the country improves its market mechanisms and adopts increasingly comprehensive reforms of the management of sea use. The market now plays a fundamental and increasingly important role in allocating sea area resources. Consequently, the market has significant leverage in the promotion of intensive and frugal use of sea area resources. The transfer of use rights is carried out in secondary markets, in which the transactions include transfers, leases, subcontracts, mortgages, and participation. These transactions are conducted using various kinds of price, such as the trading price, mortgaged price, pawn price, and requisition price. Trading price refers to the price at which the sea-use rights are auctioned, bidden, listed, transferred, and subleased. Mortgaged price refers to the price assessed for the sea-use rights mortgaged to obtain a loan. Pawn price refers to the price paid by the pawnbroker to the drawer when the latter (Qingsong Yu and Qi Lianming, 2006), as the assignee of sea-use rights, pawns the rights due to financial distress. Requisition price refers to the compensation price paid to the assignee when the government redeems the rights early.

6.3.1 *The Methods for Assessing the Value of Sea-Use Rights*

The development of the market for sea-use rights has been remarkable in recent years. In regions like Liaoning, Shandong, and Jiangsu, several bidding and auction transactions of use rights have been carried out. In cities such as Wenzhou and Qinhuangdao, secondary markets have emerged to facilitate transactions in mortgaging and joint venturing. The development and improvement of the markets have promoted the intensive and frugal use of sea area resources. The coastal reclamation projects involve large investments, a long cycle of development and construction, a high return on the sea area use rights, and drastic changes to the natural properties of the sea areas. Therefore, to assess the value of the use rights accurately, numerous factors have to be considered simultaneously, such as the project location, means of development, objectives of development, and costs. The values are currently assessed by calculating the present value of incomes, calculating the surplus, and comparing the project with similar ones in the market (Fengmin Miao, 2007).

(1) *Calculating the present earnings value*: The present earnings value method is also called the income approach or income capitalization approach. It estimates the value of an appraised asset by discounting the projected incomes of the asset to the present value. In essence, the method converts the future incomes of an asset into the asset's present value, which is deemed the revaluation value of the asset to be appraised. The revaluation value can be calculated as the sum of the expected annual income each year discounted to present values.

In China, this method is widely used for sea-area appraisal in the belief that the price of sea-area resources is the capitalization of their incomes. In applying this method, future incomes in the profitable sea-use periods need to be estimated, and an appropriate discount rate needs to be selected. Then, the price of a sea area to be used within a time horizon and under a particular property right can be calculated as the sum of the present values (on the date of appraisal), obtained by converting future incomes in the profitable sea-use periods. In general, the objective of using a sea area is to obtain the net income that can be expected under normal circumstances and to earn this income continuously in the coming years within a specific horizon. The total amount (the present value on the appraisal date) can be derived by discounting the future net incomes with an appropriate reduction interest rate. If that sum of money were deposited with a bank at an interest rate equal to the discount rate, the interest to be paid periodically would be equal to the net income. The amount of money is the theoretical price of the sea. It is evident that in appraising the price of a sea area by applying this method, it is crucial to estimate the correct future income, the number of income periods, and the reduction rate.

(2) *Residual method*: This method is also called the hypothetical development method, the residual approach, or the residual value method. It determines the price of a fixed asset as the surplus derived by deducting the construction costs, service fees related to building construction and transactions, interest, profit, and taxes from the estimated price of the property under normal conditions after the property is developed. It is an appropriate and practical valuation method. In essence, the method can be explained by the law of rent. The difference lies in the fact that the law of rent focuses on the residual of the annual land rent while the method of calculating the surplus concerns the lump sum residual of the price.

The method is mainly applicable to sea use for coastal reclamation. For this method, a sea area's price is deemed to be the surplus after deducting all the development costs from the value of the reclaimed land. For coastal reclamation projects, the transfer price of the reclaimed land, or the total income that could be earned by the rights holder (the value of reclaimed land), can be estimated by data such as (i) the transfer price of adjacent land; (ii) the benchmark price of adjacent land; (iii) the construction costs of supporting facilities; and (iv) the supporting facilities for coastal reclamation. If the reclaimed land cannot be sold and must be developed by the rights holder, the value is the cost of acquiring similar land in the adjacent area for the same development activities by assuming that the rights holder did not carry out the coastal reclamation. The income that can be earned by the rights holder can be estimated through substitution.

For this method, it is crucial to determine the land price. It can be estimated as the price of adjacent land, assuming that the land selected is of the same type. For example, if the land will be used for commercial purposes, commercial land should be selected for comparison.

(3) *Market comparison method*: This method derives the price of a sea area by identifying transactions recently closed for similar sea areas based on the substitution principle and then adjusting the price for differences in terms of transaction conditions, dates, and other specific factors. Similar sea areas here refers to a similarity in terms of regional characteristics as well as factors and conditions affecting the price (Fengmin Miao, 2004).

A precondition for using the market comparison method is an established market for trading in sea-area resources and a sufficient number of transactions. With the development of China's market, the method will be used more widely to assess the price of sea-area resources. The essential features of this method are the selection of market and transactions and adjustment for factors affecting the price.

6.3.2 *Discussions on the Suitability of the Assessment Methods for Different Sea Areas*

For reclaimed land that has not been traded, given the uncertainties in calculating the value of sea-area use rights, the cost method is suitable for assessment. This method is also suitable for land used for public buildings and facilities such as roads, pipelines, vegetation land, and parks in the regional planning of construction projects. In applying the cost method, the value of the sea-area use rights is calculated as the sum of the acquisition costs for the rights, the development costs, the interest related to the development, a reasonable profit, taxes, and gains in the value of the sea-use rights. The interest payable is calculated separately for the investments to cover the acquisition costs, development costs, and taxes for the specified periods. The taxes are calculated or adjusted per the relevant national policies. Profits can be calculated on the basis of the return on investment for similar projects in the same market. The gains are calculated by multiplying the gain rate with the sum of the acquisition costs, development costs, taxes, interest, and profits. The gain rate can be set according to the gains of adjacent land.

For reclaimed land to be used for commercial, residential, and industrial purposes, the hypothetical development method can be used to assess the value of the sea-area use rights. As mentioned before, the value is derived by deducting the following items from the value obtainable from the sea area and the buildings to be built: the cumulative costs of the coastal reclamation project, the construction project, and selling activities, as well as the ordinary profit to be earned. The total value of the real estate is subject to the type of real estate to be developed after reclamation. The market comparison method can be used to determine the value of residential buildings and industrial plants based on the transaction prices of immovable properties of similar use, nature, and structure. For office buildings and commercial real estate, the net income from leasing the property, determined by the market comparison method according to the rent level in the market for properties of a similar nature, use, structure, and condition, will be used to derive the total value by the present value method. The costs of real estate include the construction costs and service fees. The construction costs may be estimated using the method of the construction project budget. The fees are estimated by multiplying the ratio by the construction costs.

For large-scale coastal reclamation for several projects in a well-developed market for sea-area use rights, with a sufficient number of transactions of substitutable use rights, the market comparison method can be used. In applying the method, generally, three similar transactions are selected. They should be comparable and substitutable with the sea area to be assessed in having the same use, being in adjacent or similar locations, and occurring at a similar trading time. The transactions should also be compared in terms of the factors affecting the value of the rights directly.

In regions with established benchmark prices and a system of price adjustment, the value can be assessed by adjusting the benchmark prices. The benchmark prices here are the average value of sea-use rights with the longest statutory terms at a specific benchmark date for each type of sea use. The benchmark value can be expressed as a level benchmark or a district benchmark. The level benchmark is the average value of sea-area use rights at a specific level and with the longest statutory terms. The district benchmark is the average value of sea-area use rights in a specific homogeneous district and with the longest statutory terms.

6.4 Management of Requisitioned and Reserved Coastal Reclamation Resources

With its continuous development and improvement, the sea-area use rights market in China has become a meaningful way to acquire the use rights. The market is similar to the land-use rights market in that participants in both markets trade for profits. Some large participants may hoard massive rights by leveraging their deep pockets to earn excessive profits through market manipulation, which may distort the market and disrupt the regular order of sea-area resource development. Therefore, it is necessary to establish a government-led reserve of sea-area resources, which will be released to the market in a planned and systematic way by different functional uses and types. This measure could ensure that demand for sea-area resources is satisfied and that the market for sea-area use rights is developed robustly (Yan Wang *et al.*, 2014).

6.4.1 *Rationales behind the Management of Requisitioned and Reserved Coastal Reclamation Resources*

(1) *Recycling existing resources for coastal reclamation and optimizing the allocation of resources*: According to China's relevant laws and regulations on the use of sea areas, the use terms vary for different purposes. The term for construction projects is 50 years, the longest for any purpose. Without an extension, the use rights that expire will be revoked to prevent any transfer. Due to improvements in sea-salt production technologies and fluctuations in market demand, many salt farms have been abandoned or have been operated exceptionally inefficiently. This is also true for some sea areas used for aquaculture. In addition, some marginal sea areas that

have not been allocated have been idle for a long time. Due to their considerable size, these sites seriously hinder the development of sea-area resources and the development and quality of the marine economy. To this end, it is necessary to establish a government-led reserve mechanism to recover the expired use rights, requisition and reserve inefficient salt farms, consolidate and restore abandoned and inefficient aquaculture sea areas through replacement arrangements, and replace and consolidate dispersed and idle sea areas. Building on these efforts, the government could establish a reserve database for sea areas by level and type based on marine functional zoning through centralized planning and preparation. As for the reserved sea-area use rights, the transfer price will be determined by level and type by the assessment institutions. The rights will be transferred through listing, bidding, or auction in a centralized manner. The above measures for recycling existing sea-area resources could optimize the allocation of resources.

(2) *Further improving the market mechanism for sea-area use rights*: As early as 2002, the Ministry of Finance and the SOA jointly issued a document requiring regions with large market demand and highly developed sea areas to carry out bidding, auctions, and listings for rights in a planned way in order to establish an appropriate market operation mechanism for such rights. The markets have emerged in some regions. However, there are several issues to be addressed. One of the most significant issues is the lack of reserve capacity and of specialized organizations for the resources' reservation and trading to ensure that the markets operate in an open, fair, and equitable manner. Therefore, it is necessary to establish a reserve mechanism for sea-area resources. The government could facilitate the establishment of a trading mechanism in the primary market for sea-area use rights through open, fair, and equitable bidding, auctions, and listings according to marine functional zoning, sea-area use planning, and demand in the sea-area use rights market. The measure could ensure balanced and robust development of the primary market. A standardized primary market would promote the robust development of the secondary market for leasing, transfer, and mortgaging of use rights, realizing the objectives of conserving and adding to the value of national sea-area assets.

(3) *Making intensive use of the existing reclamation resources to conserve and add to the value of national sea-area assets*: Through the reserve management of sea-area resources, the government could requisition,

restore, consolidate, manage, and transfer at appropriate times the inefficient, dispersed, and dysfunctional sea areas to realize their intensive and efficient use. The government could thereby increase the use-value of the resources to conserve and add to the value of national sea-area assets and to increase the benefits of using them as assets. Through reservation, management, and transfer of the resources, the state and local governments could earn sufficient income to fund the consolidation, restoration, and protection of sea-area resources in order to form a benign circle for the management of sea-area resources. At the same time, governments can also reserve the shoreline, sea-area resources for coastal reclamation, aquaculture, and other industries or special uses, as well as rare sea resources for their efficient use, thereby supporting the sustained and rapid development of China's marine economy.

6.4.2 *China's Management Practices in the Reservation of Sea-Area Resources*

In 2010, building on forest rights reform and land reserve management methods, Putian city in Fujian Province requisitioned and reserved 2,000 hm^2 of sea in Hanjiang District and Xiuyu District for aquaculture. This was the first pilot program in China for reserving sea-area resources in terms of scope, mode, procedure, and source of funds. In January 2013, in Xiangshan County, Zhejiang successfully carried out its first open bidding for the auction of a government-reserved sea area for construction purposes. The project is being organized and implemented by the Xiangshan County Ocean and Fisheries Bureau as the No. 1 Panjitang plot in Hepu Town. A marine economic development company won the right to use the sea area at a transaction price of 25.36 million Yuan. In December 2013, Xiangshan County Ocean and Fisheries Bureau presented an application for a reserve, covering an area of 19.5038 hm^2, to Zhejiang Provincial Department of Marine and Fishery for examination and approval. In February 2014, Nantong Sea Area Reserve Center completed a sea-area reserve of 496.5 hm^2 for fisheries and a construction sea-area reserve of more than 2,670 hm^2 for projects in the Yaosha sea area.

The management system for reserves has barely emerged in China, and all the coastal areas are exploring feasible methods for reserve management. There are still many problems in the management system due to

China's current sea-area management system and insufficient recognition of the value of sea-area resources.

(1) *The function and status of sea-area resource reserve institutions is not clear*: At present, although many local governments have clarified the functions and responsibilities of sea-area reserve management institutions, their functions and status are still unclear. Some of them are directly attached to marine administrators, some are separately established public institutions, and some still perform their duties in the form of state-owned enterprises.

(2) *Shortage of management talent for sea-area resource reserves*: Management of sea-area resource reserves is a new field, and the work is rather complex. It involves sea-area resource measurement and reservation, consolidation projects, value assessment, and transfer through the market. There is a severe shortage of outstanding interdisciplinary talent with comprehensive knowledge and professional skills.

(3) *The operational mechanism for the management of sea-area resource reserves needs to be improved*: Although some local governments have run a reserve system on a trial basis, financing of the projects is rather difficult because of the large amount of funds needed for requisition, consolidation, restoration, and management, the limited financial resources of local governments, and the fact that the mortgaging of sea-area use rights is only accepted by a few financial institutions.

(4) *Insufficient guidance of state policies for the reserve management of sea-area resources*: Although some local governments have pilot projects for reserve management, a new management system requires inputs of talent, capital, and facilities. The current management system for sea-area use is still restrictive in some aspects. Macro guidance and support are needed at the national level.

6.4.3 *Discussions on a Possible Reserve Management Mode for Existing Resources for Coastal Reclamation*

The existing resources for coastal reclamation are similar to land resources in many respects. With due consideration to the specific characteristics of coastal reclamation resources, the management approaches used for land resources are also applicable. Therefore, it is possible to establish a specific reserve management mode for marine resources by building on the system for land resources.

(1) *Establish a consolidation and reserve center for existing coastal reclamation resources*: As part of the national coastal zone consolidation and restoration work, municipal sea-area resource consolidation and reserve (trading) centers could be built and managed like state-owned enterprises. With the centers being responsible for project implementation, it would be possible to separate the implementation and supervision of coastal zone consolidation and restoration projects. The centers, in performing their duties, could (1) include the sea areas in urgent need of consolidation and restoration in a national working plan and the sea areas ready for development in the reserve database, (2) make available sea-area use rights for different locations, uses, and sizes on the basis of market demand in a planned manner, and (3) divert part of the income from the transfer of rights to funding the consolidation and restoration projects that cannot be covered by local financial resources and to optimizing the mechanism for consolidation and restoration of sea-area resources.

(2) *Reserves of existing resources by type and source*: Sea-area resources should be reserved according to the requirements of the control of the use of sea space in accordance with marine functional zoning. In the agricultural and fisheries functional zones, the reserves can be implemented as sea areas enclosed for agricultural purposes, encircled sea areas, bottom planting and breeding sea areas, and sea areas for floating rafts (Wenbin Gao *et al.*, 2009). In the transportation functional zones, the reserves can be implemented by level, according to the carrying capacity of deepwater shoreline. In the industrial and urban construction functional zones, the reserves can be implemented by district according to the size of the area suitable for coastal reclamation, as well as by shape, distribution, and impact on resources and environment. The sources of the types of sea-area resource mentioned above include (a) sea areas recovered according to the law when the use rights term expires; (b) sea areas lying idle and recovered according to the law; (c) sea areas where the uses need to be adjusted to implement marine functional zoning; (d) sea areas that cannot be developed continuously after the rights holder has obtained the rights and they cannot be transferred; (e) sea areas that need to be reserved in the public

interest or to implement marine functional zoning; and (f) other sea areas in need of reservation (Anning Suo *et al.*, 2016).

(3) *Improve the value assessment of existing coastal reclamation resources and the principle of user pays*: A value assessment system for existing coastal reclamation resources in the dimensions of asset valuation and development valuation should be established in order to assess not only the assets in the form of coastal reclamation resources but also the value of developing the resources. The assessment of value provides the technical conditions for improving the primary markets for bidding, auctions, listings, and transfers. It also provides a basic pricing mechanism for the development of secondary markets for leasing, mortgaging, and participation, thereby realizing the market allocation and optimization of sea-area resources and safeguarding the implementation of the reserve system.

(4) *Implement a planned system for the reserve and supply of the existing sea-reclamation resources*: The reservation of sea-area resources should be managed in a planned manner according to the actual regional situations in the development of the sea-area resources. Specifically, after the steps of requisition, reservation, and development, the reserved sea-area resources should be supplied to the market in a planned manner according to the development of the sea area and market supply and demand for the sea-area resources. In addition, the reserved resources should be transferred through bidding, listing, and auction so as to develop the market for the circulation of sea areas. Furthermore, the reservation should be implemented according to marine functional zoning and other plans to obtain a balanced structure of various uses and to facilitate effective government macro-control of the market.

(5) *Expand the funding sources for reservation of existing coastal reclamation resources*: Reservations require a large amount of funding. In light of the less-developed mortgage market for sea-area use rights, diverse ways of raising funds should be explored. First, the national fund for current coastal zone consolidation and restoration projects can be used to restore the environment for coastal resources. That part of the restored resources that can be transferred through bidding, auction, and listing could generate a surplus, which could be used for the consolidation

and restoration of other sea-area resources. For any part that cannot be transferred readily, the consolidation and restoration of other sea-area resources could be funded with bank loans obtained by mortgaging the sea-area use rights. When the other sea-area resources are transferred, the proceeds can be used to repay the loan and then redeem the use rights. Moreover, areas of the sea reserved for aquaculture can be leased. The rent can be used to fund the requisition and reservation of sea-area resources.

(6) *Incentives for consolidation and reservation of sea-area resources*: To further expand the coverage of the pilot program for consolidation and reservation, the state and local governments could devise incentives in terms of management policies, collection of royalties, and allocation of the proceeds from transferring the use rights. The development of a benign cycle—of requisition and reservation, consolidation and restoration, and market transfer—can promote the intensive and frugal use of sea-area resources. At the national level, cities and counties that have performed well in terms of consolidation, reservation, and market transfer of sea-area resources can be recognized as model cities and counties entitled to special support in coastal zone consolidation and restoration projects. At the local level, the experience of Putian city is valuable for other local governments. Specifically, if the use rights are transferred through bidding, auction, and listing, and the proceeds are higher than the requisition costs according to national and provincial standards, 30% of the surplus will be retained by the city or county for the development of subsequent projects.

Chapter 7

Dynamic Monitoring and Evaluation of Coastal Reclamation

7.1 Sea-Use Dynamic Monitoring of Coastal Reclamation

Coastal reclamation is a large-scale marine development activity, with massive investment and substantial impact on the marine ecological environment and the use of the sea. Effective sea-use dynamic monitoring of coastal reclamation projects is critical to enhancing coastal reclamation management, regulating sea-use and construction activities, conserving marine resources, and protecting the ecological environment (Xiaoying Hu *et al.*, 2009; Ling Zhu, and Liu Baiqiao, 2009).

7.1.1 *Purposes and Scope of Sea-Use Dynamic Monitoring of Coastal Reclamation*

Sea-use dynamic monitoring of coastal reclamation aims to: (1) provide a full picture of how the reclamation construction process is conducted and how a specific sea area is developed, (2) identify and prevent in a timely manner any significant adverse impact caused by the construction process on the surrounding marine resources and environment, and (3) cover the whole sea-use cycle of the coastal reclamation project, that is, before, during, and after its implementation.

For the coastal reclamation management, sea-use dynamic surveillance and monitoring are carried out in four stages: the application for approval stage, construction stage, final sea-sue acceptance stage, and post-evaluation stage (Xuping Bao *et al.*, 2014).

(1) *Monitoring during the application for approval stage*: This monitoring stage extends from the application for a coastal reclamation project to the receipt of its approval. It covers (a) how the project site is developed (including an investigation to determine whether any development activities are taking place before permission has been granted); (b) how the surrounding sea areas are developed; (c) the relationship between the project and the shoreline to be occupied (especially the status and occupancy of the natural shoreline); (d) the project's compliance with marine functional zoning; (e) the accuracy in defining the project's site and area; and (f) the exclusiveness of ownership of sea-use rights.

(2) *Monitoring during the construction stage*: Monitoring during this stage occurs from the beginning of construction, after the acquisition of the necessary approvals and certificates for the sea-use rights, to the completion of construction for the coastal reclamation project. It covers (a) how the sea is used, including project location, uses of the sea, area of sea used, ownership, sea-use scope, sea-use approach, spatial distribution, and layout design; and (b) the status of the project, such as the overall construction progress in sea enclosure and land reclamation and the specific construction technologies and methods employed.

(3) *Monitoring during the final sea-use acceptance stage*: Monitoring during this stage, from the completion of the coastal reclamation project to its final sea-use acceptance, covers (a) the property line and area of the sea actually used; (b) the actual sea-use areas; (c) the demolition of temporary facilities; and (d) the natural shoreline occupied and artificial shoreline created.

(4) *Monitoring during the post-evaluation stage*: Monitoring during this stage takes place from the time of final sea-use acceptance to several years after the project is put into operation. It mainly covers (a) actual development in the project area; (b) whether the uses of the project area deviate from the intended uses without proper authorization; (c) the significant long-term impact of the project on the surrounding marine ecological environment; and (d) the project's social and economic benefits.

7.1.2 *Methods for the Sea-Use Dynamic Monitoring of Coastal Reclamation*

The scope and requirements of sea-use dynamic monitoring vary in the different stages. Accordingly, various monitoring methods are employed (Yuanbin Fu *et al.*, 2009). Monitoring during the application for approval stage mainly takes the form of remote sensing and systematic review, which are supplemented by on-site monitoring. During the construction stage, a method of combining remote sensing, on-site monitoring, and video monitoring is adopted. In the final sea-use acceptance stage, on-site monitoring is the main method, and in the post-evaluation stage, monitoring mainly involves data collection, field investigation and survey, and remote sensing. Figure 7.1 presents the workflow of the sea-use dynamic monitoring of coastal reclamation.

(1) *Methods for sea-use monitoring during the application for approval stage*: The sea-use monitoring of the current status of the project site involves both on-site monitoring and satellite remote sensing image monitoring. For the technical review of a project's application forms, the basic operational module in the management system for national sea-use dynamic surveillance and monitoring is used. Data for the property line of the sea area requested by the application, ownership of the adjacent sea areas, and marine functional zoning are overlaid onto the latest high spatial resolution remote sensing images (Anning Suo and Minghui Zhang, 2015). Key aspects of monitoring include the accuracy of the property line and area defined in the application, ownership conflicts between the application sea-use area and adjacent sea areas, compliance with marine functional zoning, the location of the project site in relation to the shoreline and how the shoreline is occupied, and incidents of development without appropriate authorization. For any such incidents identified, past remote sensing image data will be retrieved to determine the construction time of the project, and the development of adjacent sea areas will also become the subject of monitoring.

(2) *Method for sea-use monitoring during the construction stage*: Sea-use monitoring in this stage mainly takes the form of remote sensing and on-site monitoring, which are supplemented by remote video monitoring. The frequency of monitoring can be adjusted according to the construction progress of the coastal reclamation project. Generally, on-site monitoring should be carried out every quarter. However, it is also needed at

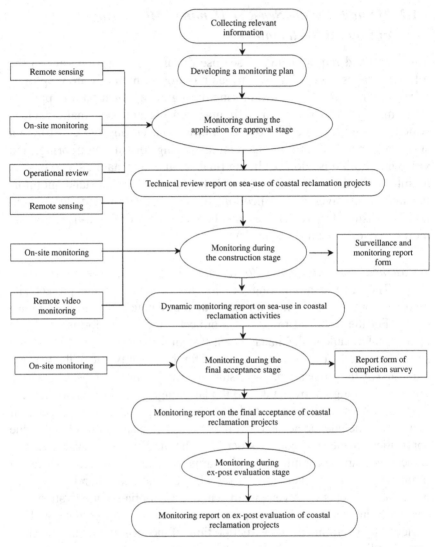

Figure 7.1   Workflow of the dynamic monitoring of coastal reclamation activities.

key construction milestones, such as the beginning of construction, the closure of the cofferdam, and the completion of major works for coastal reclamation. Remote sensing monitoring requires the timely acquisition of the latest remote sensing images from satellites, aircraft, or unmanned aerial vehicles (UAVs). At least one batch of images with a spatial resolution of no less than 15–30 m is required every quarter, and at least one batch of high-precision images better than 5 m is required every year. For key coastal reclamation projects, one batch of UAV images is required every year. On-site monitoring mainly involves the use of a Real-Time Kinematic (RTK) apparatus and other survey equipment to measure the position of points along the property line and the elevation of the dam or the land reclaimed. Pictures of the project site are also taken. For projects with remote video monitoring facilities, the facilities should be used to update information on developments in constructing the coastal reclamation projects. The recording forms of remote video monitoring should be completed periodically. The information to be recorded includes construction methods, materials used, construction progress, the impact on surrounding marine functional zones, and the safety hazards identified.

Quarterly monitoring focuses on conformance with the requirements set out by the approval documents in terms of developments in construction, the extent of the sea used, area of the sea used, how the sea is used, actual usage, construction technologies, and construction methods; the impact on adjacent sea usage and marine functional zoning; and the implementation of management measures for sea-use. Annual monitoring mainly involves identifying the extent of sea-use by extracting information from remote sensing images. The information is used to prepare special drawings for the remote sensing monitoring of coastal reclamation projects. The drawings are marked by a red line for sea-use and a green line for construction to calculate the area of enclosed sea, the area of reclaimed land, and the area of the sea used temporarily. Using the calculated area, it is possible to identify issues such as sea-use beyond the designated extent or area and changes in the location of sea-use without appropriate authorization.

Suspected or actual non-compliance with sea-use requirements should be reported by the monitoring organization in a timely manner to the marine administrator at the same administrative level. On the basis of information such as monitoring data, videos, and images, the marine administrator should hold an interview with the corporate representative of the project to notify the potential hazards and the necessary emergency measures, as well as advice on how to use the sea area in a scientific and normative manner. As for confirmed non-compliance, the monitoring organization should report to the marine administrator at the same administrative level in a timely manner and escalate the issue to the approving authority of the coastal reclamation project through the management system for national sea-use dynamic surveillance and monitoring.

(3) *Methods for monitoring during the final sea-use acceptance stage*: After the completion of a coastal reclamation project, an on-site survey is carried out. It can be implemented together with the final sea-use acceptance survey as appropriate. The points along the actual property line are measured by RTK or other surveying equipment on the site. Pictures of the project site are also taken. The on-site survey mainly covers conformance with the requirements set out by the approval of registration in terms of the location of the sea area used by the project, uses of the enclosed sea and structures, area of the sea used, coordinates of the actual property line, and how the sea is used; whether the shoreline is occupied beyond the scope determined by the approval of registration; the natural shoreline occupied and the artificial shoreline created; the demolition of temporary facilities; implementation of key target security measures and risk mitigation measures; and whether the project has a considerable adverse impact on adjacent sea-use activities and marine functional zones.

(4) *Methods for sea-use monitoring during the post-evaluation stage*: The sea-use monitoring during this stage mainly involves remote sensing, data collection, and on-site survey and investigation. It covers the actual development on the reclaimed land, including whether the actual uses of each sea-use unit have been changed without proper authorization; the area of reclaimed land; the floor area; the development of administrative office buildings, vegetation, and roads; and whether the surrounding shoreline has problems with corrosion or deposition. The key data collected about the coastal reclamation project comprise information on social benefits, economic benefits, and risk prevention. In terms of economic benefits, the indicators include project investment, output, earnings, and taxes paid. In terms of social benefits, the indicators include employment, income, education, and health care.

7.2 Sea-Use Dynamic Evaluation of Coastal Reclamation

The sea-use dynamic evaluation of coastal reclamation involves analysis and evaluation of the sea-use dynamic monitoring data with the aim of presenting a report to ocean administrators in an intuitive and clear manner. The evaluation covers compliance in terms of functional positioning, spatial distribution, and layout design; compliance in terms of area, scope, and construction progress; the treatment of stakeholders; and the various management measures implemented (Derui Song *et al.*, 2012; Houjun Wang *et al.*, 2015).

7.2.1 *Evaluation of Compliance in Terms of Functional Positioning, Spatial Distribution, and Layout Design*

This evaluation concerns the compliance of project implementation with project planning in three respects, which will be discussed in detail in what follows. For an accurate evaluation, quantified indicators are used on a trial basis.

For functional positioning, the compliance scores are either 1.00 for compliance or 0 for non-compliance for each of the planned functional zones. The weight for each is the total weight of 1.00 divided by the number of functional zones. For example, in a project with five functional zones, if three of them, as implemented, comply with the planned function positioning, the value assign is $0.20 \times 1.00 + 0.20 \times 1.00 + 0.20 \times 1.00 + 0.20 \times 0 + 0.20 \times 0 = 0.60$.

For spatial distribution, the compliance scores are either 1.00 for compliance or 0 for non-compliance for each of the originally planned functional zones. The weight for each is the total weight of 1.00 divided by the number of functional zones.

In terms of layout design, the compliance of the project as implemented with the original project planning can be evaluated on the basis of six indicators: (1) the intensity index of coastal reclamation, (2) index of shoreline gain or loss, (3) index of seafront shoreline, (4) efficient use of the natural shoreline, (5) plot ratio of the water area, and (6) index of marine passages. The value-assignment method is shown in Table 7.1. For full compliance, the value assigned is 1.00; for 80% compliance, the value is 0.80; for 60% compliance, it is 0.60; and so on. For the weights of the above indicators and their quantification methods, see the book, *Assessing Methodologies for Coastal Reclamation* by Yonghai Yu and Anning Suo in 2013.

7.2.2 *Evaluation of Compliance in Terms of Area, Scope, and Construction Progress*

This evaluation concerns the compliance of project implementation with project planning in three respects, which will be discussed in detail in what follows.

Table 7.1   Evaluation of compliance in terms of functional positioning.

Indicator	Ratio of targets reached (%)	Value assigned	Weight
Intensity index of coastal reclamation	100	1.00	0.20
Index of shoreline gain or loss	80	0.80	0.20
Index of seafront shoreline	60	0.60	0.20
Efficient use of natural shoreline	40	0.40	0.20
Plot ratio of water area	20	0.20	0.10
Index of marine passages	0	0	0.10

Evaluation of area compliance covers the construction and reserved water areas. In comparing the area as planned and as built, a score of 1.00 is given for complete compliance, a score of 0.80 is given for an area 20% less or more than the planned area, a score of 0.60 is given for an area 40% less or more, a score of 0.40 is given for an area 60% less or more, a score of 0.20 is given for an area 80% less or more, and a score of 0 is given for an area over 100% less or more.

Evaluation of scope compliance mainly refers to the consistency in geographical location or how the project location as built has deviated from the original plan. The values are assigned according to the following method. The value for complete consistency is 1.00; in cases where the area of deviated spatial scope accounts for 0.10% of the total area, the value is 0.90; if the area accounts for 0.20% of the total, the value is 0.80; and so on. When 1.0% of the spatial scope deviates from the plan, the value is 0.

Evaluation of construction progress compliance mainly refers to compliance with the planned progress. It is evaluated at several construction stages as designed, and each stage has a weight of $1/n$. For each of the stages, the value assigned to full compliance is 1.00; for 20% expedition or delay, the value is 0.80; for 40% expedition or delay, it is 0.60; and so on (see Table 7.2).

7.2.3 *Evaluation of the Treatment of Stakeholders*

This evaluation targets the impact on stakeholders. The values are assigned according to the following criteria. If the stakeholders are well treated without petitions or incidents related to conflict of interests, the

Table 7.2 Evaluation of compliance in terms of area, scope, and construction progress.

Secondary indicator	Proportion of compliance (%)	Value assigned	Weight	Primary indicator	Value	Weight
Area compliance in coastal reclamation	100	1.00	0.50	Area compliance	0.80	0.40
Compliance in area of water	80	0.80	0.50			
Scope compliance in coastal reclamation	0.10	0.90	0.50	Scope compliance	0.85	0.40
Scope compliance in water	0.20	0.80	0.50			
Progress compliance in the first stage	80	0.90	0.30	Progress compliance	0.94	0.20
Progress compliance in the second stage	90	0.90	0.30			
Progress compliance in the third stage	100	1.00	0.40			

value assigned is 1.00. In cases of petitions being submitted to the relevant authority on the county level, the value is 0.80. In cases of petitions being submitted to the relevant authority at the city, provincial, or national level, the values are 0.60, 0.40, and 0.20, respectively. If there are casualties due to a conflict of interest, the value is 0 (see Table 7.3). The weight of the petitioning event is the reciprocal of the number of stakeholders n ($1/n$). For example, for a coastal reclamation project that involves five stakeholders, if two of them are poorly treated and submit a petition at the provincial level and one submits a petition at the national level, the score will be $0.40 \times 0.20 + 0.40 \times 0.20 + 0 \times 0.20 + 0 \times 0.20 \times 0.20 = 0.20$.

7.2.4 *Evaluation of the Implementation of Management Measures for Coastal Reclamation*

This evaluation covers the implementation of measures for sea-use dynamic monitoring, marine environmental impact monitoring, environmental management, final sea-use acceptance, and establishment of the environmental threshold.

Table 7.3 Evaluation treatment of the stakeholders of a coastal reclamation project.

Level of conflict of interest	Scope of conflict of interest	Value assigned
1	Stakeholders are well treated without petitions or incidents related to conflict of interests	1.00
2	Petitions are submitted at the county level	0.80
3	Petitions are submitted at the city level	0.60
4	Petitions are submitted at the provincial level	0.40
5	Petitions are submitted at the national level	0.20
6	Heavy casualties due to conflict of interests	0

For the sea-use dynamic monitoring measures, the following criteria are used for evaluation. If the sea-use dynamic monitoring is carried out throughout the implementation of the coastal reclamation project and the evaluation report on sea-use dynamic monitoring is prepared, the value assigned is 1.00. Without sea-use dynamic monitoring, the value is 0; with sea-use dynamic monitoring covering half of the project cycle, the value is 0.50.

For measures monitoring the impact on the marine environment, the following criteria are used for evaluation. If tracking and monitoring are carried out throughout the implementation of the coastal reclamation project and the evaluation report on the tracking and monitoring of the marine environmental impact is prepared, the value assigned is 1.00. Without such tracking and monitoring, the value is 0; with tracking and monitoring covering half of the cycle, the value is 0.50.

For the environmental management measures, several criteria are used for evaluation. The sea-use demonstration report and the marine environmental impact evaluation report for coastal reclamation projects and the regional sea-use planning for construction projects suggest several environmental management measures. When the environmental management planning is developed and management measures under the planning are implemented according to the suggested measures, the value assigned is 1.00, providing the measures prevent environmental issues. For environmental issues caused by a failure to implement environmental management measures suggested by the demonstration report, the value is

0. For environmental issues caused by the loose implementation of the measures under the environmental management planning, the value is 0.50. When a partial environmental management plan is developed and management measures under the plan are implemented, the value is $1/n$ if there are no environmental issues, with n being the number of measures suggested by the demonstration report.

For the implementation of final sea-use acceptance measures, the following criteria are used for evaluation. For a coastal reclamation project, when the final sea-use acceptance report is developed, the value assigned is 1.00; when there is no final sea-use acceptance, the value is 0.

For coastal reclamation projects, the environmental threshold is evaluated according to the following criteria. When a high environmental threshold set and applied strictly on potential occupants prevents marine environmental pollution issues, the value assigned is 1.00. Where there is a threshold, even a high one, that is not strictly applied on potential occupants and the marine environment is slightly polluted as a result, the value is 0.80. Where there is a high threshold that is not applied strictly and serious marine environmental pollution ensues, the value is 0.60. When there is no environmental threshold on potential occupants and, consequently, mild pollution occurs in the marine environment, the value is 0.40. If severe pollution is caused due to the lack of a threshold, the value is 0.20. In the case of catastrophic pollution caused by the lack of a threshold, the value is 0 (see Table 7.4).

7.3 Tracking and Monitoring of the Marine Environmental Impact for Coastal Reclamation

Coastal reclamation projects may have a considerable impact on the marine environment, affecting the marine hydrodynamic and erosion/siltation conditions, marine ecological environment, and the environment for fishery resources, for example. To identify and mitigate the impact in a timely manner during the construction of coastal reclamation projects, some ocean administrators require that the tracking and monitoring of the impact be carried out during construction (Shuquan Chen, 2009). However, there has been no systematic and formal method for evaluating the results from tracking and monitoring. In this section, we attempt to build an evaluation framework for this purpose (Zong-en Hu and Wang Miao, 2016).

Table 7.4 Evaluating the implementation of management measures for coastal reclamation projects.

Management measure	Implementation	Value assigned	Weight
Dynamic monitoring of sea-use	Dynamic monitoring of sea-use is carried out	1.00	0.20
	Dynamic monitoring of sea-use is carried out for half of the project cycle	0.50	
	Dynamic monitoring of sea-use is not carried out	0	
Tracking and monitoring of marine environmental impact	Tracking and monitoring of marine environmental impact are carried out	1.00	0.20
	Tracking and monitoring of marine environmental impact are carried out for half of the project cycle	0.50	
	Tracking and monitoring of marine environmental impact are not carried out	0	
Environmental management measures	There are no environmental issues because an environmental management plan is developed and management measures under the plan are implemented	1.00	0.20
	Environmental issues occur due to loose implementation of the environmental management plan developed	0.50	
	The environmental management plan is developed and partially implemented and there are no environmental issues	$1/n$	
	There are environmental issues caused by failure to develop an environmental management plan and to implement the environmental management measures suggested by the demonstration report	0	

Final sea-use acceptance	The final acceptance of the coastal reclamation project has been carried out and the final acceptance report has been prepared	1.00	0.20
	The final acceptance of the coastal reclamation project has not been carried out	0	
Environmental threshold	A high environmental threshold set and strictly applied on potential occupants prevents issues of marine environmental pollution	1.00	0.20
	Threshold is not strictly applied on occupants and, consequently, the marine environment is slightly polluted	0.80	
	Threshold is not strictly applied on potential occupants and consequently the marine environment is seriously polluted	0.60	
	There is no environmental threshold on potential occupants and, consequently, mild pollution occurs to the marine environment	0.40	
	There is no environmental threshold on potential occupants and, consequently, severe pollution occurs to the marine environment	0.20	
	There is no environmental threshold on potential occupants and, consequently, catastrophic pollution occurs to the marine environment	0	

7.3.1 *A technical Framework for Evaluating the Results from Tracking and Monitoring of the Environmental Impact of Coastal Reclamation*

Given the characteristic environmental impact from coastal reclamation projects and the requirements of impact management, we adopted an analytic hierarchy process to build the framework. It comprises the following levels: goals, criteria, factors, and indicators.

(1) *Goals*: This level presents a comprehensive evaluation index, comprising the evaluation results of a comprehensive monitoring program for the environmental impact of coastal reclamation activities. As the highest level in the system of indicators, it provides an overall picture of the environmental impact. Specifically, it combines the results produced by the criteria, factors, and indicators levels through the employment of the systematic analysis process. The comprehensive evaluation index derived from evaluating the three criteria-level compound indicators can be classified into different performance grades according to the index values.

(2) *Criteria*: The criteria level provides further description of the goal level. It comprises three compound indicators: dynamic monitoring of (i) marine hydrodynamic and erosion/siltation conditions; (ii) impact on marine biological community; and (iii) impact on coastal wetland habitat.

(3) *Factor level*: The factor level is the bridge connecting the criteria and the indicator levels. It defines and clarifies the goal level and defines the scope of the indicator level. The compound indicator for tracking and monitoring marine hydrodynamic and erosion/siltation conditions comprises the monitoring indicators for marine hydrodynamic conditions and shoreline erosion/siltation conditions. The compound indicator for evaluating the results of tracking and monitoring the impact on the marine biological community comprises the monitoring indicators for the intertidal biological community, benthic biological community, and nekton community. The compound indicator for evaluating the results of tracking and monitoring the impact on coastal wetland habitat comprises the monitoring indicators for the integrity of the coastal wetland habitat, for landscape diversity in coastal wetland, and for the quality of the coastal wetland habitat.

(4) *Indicator level*: Indicators on this level refer to the variables that have clear definitions, that can be calculated directly, or that can be derived from statistical data. This level is composed by the most basic elements in the system of indicators for evaluating the results of tracking and monitoring the environmental impact of coastal reclamation activities. The selection of indicators included in this level is determined on the basis of the objectives of the evaluation, the principle of indicator selection, the existing system of indicators worldwide, the monitoring capacity, and the opinions of experts. The compound indicator for tracking and monitoring marine hydrodynamic and erosion/siltation conditions comprises the tidal prime, water exchange period, flood current velocity, ebb current velocity, coastal current velocity, coastal erosion rate, coastal erosion depth, and coastal deposition. The compound indicator for evaluating the results of tracking and monitoring the impact on the marine biological community comprises community density, the biodiversity index, the species dominance index, the species richness index, and community biomass. The compound indicator for evaluating the results of tracking and monitoring the impact on coastal wetland habitat comprises the area change index for the coastal wetland, naturalness index of the coastal wetland, landscape diversity index of the coastal wetland, landscape fragmentation index of the coastal wetland, and sediment-environment quality index of the coastal wetland. Figure 7.2 presents the framework for the system of indicators for evaluating the results of tracking and monitoring the environmental impact of coastal reclamation activities.

7.3.2 *Technical Methods for Evaluating the Results from Tracking and Monitoring the Environmental Impact of Coastal Reclamation Projects*

(1) *The compound indicator for tracking and monitoring marine hydrodynamic and erosion/siltation conditions*: Large-scale coastal reclamation activities' impact on these conditions can be well captured by changes in the marine hydrodynamic processes and the interaction between seawater and sediments.

The dynamic monitoring stations for marine hydrodynamic and erosion/siltation conditions are arranged to extend 5 km along the main flow on both sides and 2 km along the line vertical to the main flow on both sides. In principle, there should be no less than three hydrological

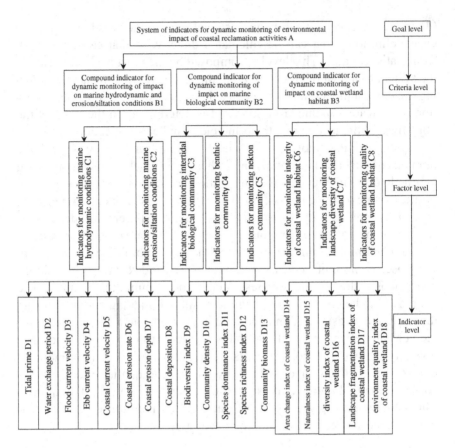

Figure 7.2   System of indicators for the dynamic monitoring of the environmental impact of coastal reclamation activities.

observation stations—one on the project site, one on the upstream, and one on the downstream. The monitoring should be conducted once every six months after the completion of the coastal reclamation project. In principle, it should be carried out during spring tides at high- or low-water periods. Hydrologic and sediment monitoring should be carried out for coastal reclamation projects with a sea area greater than 50 hm². For projects smaller than 50 hm², whether the monitoring is carried out will depend on the characteristics of the natural environment of the sea area and the form of land reclamation.

With regard to the monitoring of suspended sediment, dynamic monitoring is needed for suspended sediment from the cofferdam or the overflow mouth in dredging and blowing operations. The monitoring scope should be no less than the impact scope predicted by the original sea-use demonstration. The monitoring cycle is once a month for cofferdam construction and dredging operations. It should be once every two months for the overflow mouth in dredging and blowing operations.

The schedule for evaluating indicators for hydrodynamic and erosion/siltation conditions is shown in Table 7.5.

(2) *Indicators for monitoring the biological community*: The impacts of coastal reclamation activities on marine biological communities mainly involve the impacts on community density, biomass, biodiversity, and species dominance. To facilitate the comparison of the indicators, the biomass loss rate, number of biological species, and number of dominant species are selected for monitoring. The ecologically sensitive zones that could be affected by coastal reclamation activities include the zones under national protection for mangroves, seaweeds, and coral reef; the zones of spawning and breeding for important species; and other important biological zones. For these zones, the ecologically sensitive index is constructed. For marine biological community monitoring techniques, see Part 6, Marine Biological Survey; Part 9, Code for Marine Ecological Survey, *Code for Marine Survey*; and Part 7, Ecological Survey and Biological Monitoring for Nearshore Marine Pollution, *Code for Marine Monitoring*. The scope of the survey is defined by the sea-use demonstration. The survey is carried out in two legs for spring (May) and fall (August) of every year. Table 7.6 shows the indicators and criteria for ecological evaluation.

Table 7.5   Indicators and criteria for the evaluating impact on hydrodynamic and erosion/siltation conditions.

Indicator	Criteria (%)	Notes	Evaluation index
Decrease in the indicators for hydrodynamic and erosion/siltation conditions (≤)	2	Criteria can be adjusted according to the sensitive characteristics of the marine ecological environment and the size of environmental capacity	0.54
	5		0.27
	8		0.15

Table 7.6   Indicators and criteria for ecological evaluation.

Indicators	Criteria	Calculation method and note	Evaluation index
Biomass loss rate (%)	≤2	Calculated as the ratio of benthic biomass loss caused by coastal reclamation activities to the total benthic biomass in the whole bay	0.75
	≤5		0.39
	≤10		0.21
Biodiversity index	≤1	Shannon–Weaver index is used and the highest value in the sea area selected	0.75
	>1		0.39
	>2		0.21
Species dominance index	Disappearance of dominant species	—	0.75
	≤1	—	0.39
		—	0.21
	>2	—	0.75
	≤1	—	0.39
		—	0.21

(3) *Indicators for monitoring the wetland*: The impact of coastal reclamation activities on coastal wetland can be mainly represented by the occupation of and damage to coastal wetland that cause the shrinkage of wetland area, fragmentation of a block, monotonousness in terms of type, or a considerable increase in artificial features. To represent the impact, the landscape diversity index, landscape fragmentation index, area change index of coastal wetland, naturalness index of coastal wetland, and sediment-environment quality index of coastal wetland are used. The above indicators can be calculated as follows:

(i) *Fragmentation index for wetland blocks*:

$$FS = 1 - 1/ASI \qquad (7.1)$$

$$ASI = \sum_{i=1}^{N} A(i)\,\text{SI}(i)\big/A \qquad (7.2)$$

$$SI(i) = P(i)/\left[4\sqrt{A(i)}\right] \qquad (7.3)$$

$$A = \sum_{i=1}^{N} A(i), \qquad (7.4)$$

where *FS* is the fragmentation index for the block shape of the type of wetland, ASI is the average shape index calculated with the weight of area of the wetland block, $SI(i)$ is the shape index for wetland block i, $P(i)$ is the perimeter for wetland block i, $A(i)$ is the area for wetland block i, A is the total area for the wetland type, and N denotes the number of blocks for the wetland type.

(ii) *Naturalness index of the wetland*: The naturalness of the wetland is the naturalness of the coastal wetland in comparison with the original wetland. It is calculated as

$$W_i = \frac{\sum_{i=1}^{n} A(i)}{\sum_{i=1}^{n} A_0(i)}, \qquad (7.5)$$

where W_i is the naturalness index for Type i coastal wetland, $A(i)$ is the total area of Type i coastal wetland, and $A_0(i)$ is the original area of Type i coastal wetland.

(iii) *Index of landscape diversity*: Diversity refers to the complexity of various types of wetland within the scope of the wetland. It can be represented by the following index:

$$HYDI = -\sum_{i=1}^{m} \left[P_i \ln(P_i)\right]. \qquad (7.6)$$

That is, the ratio of each type of wetland to the total area of coastal wetland is multiplied by its logarithm; the product is then summed up and the logarithm of the sum is taken, where P_i is the ratio of Type i wetland to the total wetland area and m is the total number of wetland types. The value range for *HYDI* is HYDI ≥ 0 without upper limit. Table 7.7 summarizes the values assigned for the above indicators.

Table 7.7   Indicators and criteria for wetland evaluation.

Indicator	Range of the threshold value	Value assigned	Definition
Changes of index of landscape diversity	≥1.50	0.80	The coastal reclamation activities have increased the landscape diversity of the coastal wetland substantially
	1.50–1.00	0.50	The coastal reclamation activities have increased the landscape diversity of the coastal wetland
	<0.80	0.20	The coastal reclamation activities have decreased the landscape diversity of the coastal wetland
Changes of landscape fragmentation index	<1.00	0.80	The coastal reclamation activities have improved the landscape fragmentation of the coastal wetland
	1.20–1.00	0.60	The coastal reclamation activities have had no substantial effects on the landscape fragmentation of the coastal wetland
	≥1.20	0.20	The coastal reclamation activities have worsened the landscape fragmentation of the coastal wetland
Changes of naturalness index of wetland	≥1.20	0.80	The coastal reclamation activities have increased the area of the natural wetland considerably
	1.20–0.80	0.60	The coastal reclamation activities have had no substantial effects on the natural wetland
	<0.80	0.20	The coastal reclamation activities have decreased the area of the natural wetland considerably
Changes of area index of wetland	≥0.70	0.80	The coastal reclamation activities have caused a small shrinkage of the wetland area
	0.40–0.70	0.50	The coastal reclamation activities have caused a large shrinkage of the wetland area
	<0.40	0.20	The coastal reclamation activities have caused substantial shrinkage of the wetland area
Changes of sediment-environment quality index of wetland	≥0.80	1.00	The coastal reclamation activities have had a small effect on the sediment-environment quality of the wetland
	0.30–0.80	0.60	The coastal reclamation activities have had a large effect on the sediment-environment quality of the wetland
	<0.30	0.20	The coastal reclamation activities have had substantial effects on the sediment-environment quality of the wetland

7.3.3 Model for Evaluating the Results from the Tracking and Monitoring of the Environmental Impact of Coastal Reclamation Projects

On the basis of Figure 7.2, we can calculate the comprehensive indicator for evaluating the results from the tracking and monitoring of the environmental impact of coastal reclamation activities.

$$E_{\text{recl}} = H + C + E, \tag{7.7}$$

where E_{recl} is the comprehensive indicator, H is the indicator for tracking and monitoring the impact on marine hydrodynamic and erosion/siltation conditions, C is the indicator for tracking and monitoring the impact on the marine biological community, and E is the indicator for tracking and monitoring the impact on the coastal wetland habitat.

The comprehensive evaluation indicator E_{recl} ranges from 0 to 1.00. When $E_{\text{recl}} \geq 0.75$, it indicates that coastal reclamation projects have a serious impact on the marine environment, designated a Category III impact. When $0.75 > E_{\text{recl}} \geq 0.55$, it indicates that coastal reclamation projects have a non-negligible impact on the marine environment, or a Category II impact. When $E_{\text{recl}} < 0.55$, it indicates that coastal reclamation projects have only a slight impact on the marine environment, or a Category I impact.

The indicator for tracking and monitoring the impact on marine hydrodynamic and erosion/siltation conditions can be calculated according to the following equation:

$$H = \sum_{k=1}^{6} w_k \sum_{j=1}^{n} q_j \sum_{i=1}^{m} p_i G_i, \tag{7.8}$$

where H is the indicator for tracking and monitoring the impact on marine hydrodynamic and erosion/siltation conditions, w_k is the weight of the kth evaluation criterion, q_j is the weight of the jth evaluation factor, p_i is the weight of the ith evaluation indicator, and G_i is the value assigned for the ith evaluation indicator. Table 7.8 summarizes the indicators for each level and their weights.

Table 7.8 Weights of indicators for the environmental impact of coastal reclamation activities.

Goals level	Factors level	Weight	Indicators level	Weight
Indicator for tracking and monitoring impact on marine hydrodynamic and erosion/siltation conditions B1	Indicators for monitoring marine hydrodynamic conditions C1	0.574 2	Tidal prime index D1	0.218 8
			Water exchange period index D2	0.226 5
			Flood current velocity D3	0.181 2
			Ebb current velocity D4	0.215 7
			Coastal current velocity D5	0.157 8
	Indicators for monitoring marine erosion/siltation conditions C2	0.425 8	Coastal erosion rate D6	0.346 9
			Coastal erosion depth D7	0.251 7
			Coastal deposition D8	0.437 4
Indicator for tracking and monitoring impact on marine biological community B2	Indicators for monitoring intertidal biological community C4	0.276 0	Biodiversity index D9	0.221 7
			Community density D10	0.190 2
			Species dominance index D11	0.205 8
			Species richness index D12	0.197 2
			Community biomass D13	0.185 1
	Indicators for monitoring benthic community C5	0.386 2	Community density D14	0.190 2
			Biodiversity index D15	0.221 7
			Species richness index D16	0.197 2
			Species dominance index	0.205 8
			Community biomass	0.185 1
	Indicators for monitoring nekton community C6	0.337 8	Community density D17	0.190 2
			Biodiversity index D18	0.221 7
			Species richness index D19	0.197 2
			Species dominance index	0.205 8
			Community biomass	0.185 1
Indicator for tracking and monitoring impact on coastal wetland B3	Indicators for monitoring integrity of coastal wetland habitat C7	0.317 2	Area change index of coastal wetland D20	0.491 1
			Naturalness index of coastal wetland D21	0.508 9
	Indicators for monitoring landscape diversity of coastal wetland C8	0.289 5	Landscape diversity index of coastal wetland D22	0.557 3
			Landscape fragmentation index of coastal wetland D23	0.442 7
	Indicators for monitoring quality of coastal wetland habitat	0.393 3	Sediment-environment quality index of coastal wetland	1.00

(Left margin, vertical text:) System of indicators for tracking and monitoring impact on marine ecological environment from coastal reclamation activities A

The indicator for tracking and monitoring the impact on the marine biological community can be calculated according to the following equation:

$$C = \sum_{k=1}^{2} r_k \sum_{j=1}^{n} l_j \sum_{i=1}^{m} z_i G_i, \qquad (7.9)$$

where C is the indicator for tracking and monitoring the impact on the marine biological community from coastal reclamation activities, r_k is the weight of the kth evaluation criterion, l_j is the weight of the jth evaluation factor, z_i is the weight of the ith evaluation indicator, and G_i is the value assigned for the ith evaluation indicator. Table 7.8 summarizes the indicators for each level and their weights.

The indicator for tracking and monitoring the impact on the coastal wetland habitat can be calculated according to the following equation:

$$E = \sum_{k=1}^{2} a_k \sum_{j=1}^{n} b_j \sum_{i=1}^{m} d_i G_i, \tag{7.10}$$

where E is the indicator for tracking and monitoring the impact on the coastal wetland habitat from coastal reclamation activities, a_k is the weight of the kth evaluation criterion, b_j is the weight of the jth evaluation factor, d_i is the weight of the ith evaluation indicator, and G_i is the value assigned for the ith evaluation indicator. Table 7.8 summarizes the indicators for each level and their weights.

Chapter 8

Techniques for Final Sea-Use Acceptance of Coastal Reclamation Projects

8.1 Overview of Final Sea-Use Acceptance of Coastal Reclamation Projects

The final sea-use acceptance of coastal reclamation projects refers to the ocean administrators' comprehensive inspection and acceptance of the projects upon their completion in relation to the property line and sea-use area of coastal reclamation completed by the use-rights holders, compliance with the relevant national technical standards and specifications, and implementation of the management requirements for the sea-use (Su Liu and Zhi Jiangyu, 2016). Final sea-use acceptance is a mandated step before application to a land administrator for the land-use rights certificate for the reclaimed land. Through this step, ocean administrators can oversee and manage coastal reclamation activities effectively. It is also an important part of the national ocean and land management systems (Qinbang Sun *et al.*, 2015).

Article XXXII of the Law of the People's Republic of China on the Administration of the Use of Sea Areas stipulates that "Land reclaimed after the completion of the coastal reclamation project is the property of the state. Sea-use rights holders should apply for land registration with land administrators above the county level by presenting the sea-use rights certificate within the three months following the date of completion. Their land-use rights are confirmed by the use rights certificate for state-owned land after government above the county level registers the rights and has ordered the issuance of the certificate." To enforce the law and to build a technical framework for sea-use acceptance, the SOA has issued several supporting regulations and specifications, including the Registration of Sea-use Rights, Sea-use Acceptance Management after Coastal Reclamation Project Completion, and Specifications for Surveying Areas of Sea Use Project.

Sea-use acceptance is implemented according to the principle of "assigning responsibilities to different administrative levels and locations." That is, the SOA is responsible for overseeing the final sea-use acceptance of coastal reclamation projects nationwide and for carrying out sea-use acceptance of projects approved by the State Council. The ocean administrators at the province level (or the autonomous region/municipality directly under the central government) are responsible for the sea-use acceptance of projects approved by their local governments. The SOA and province-level ocean administrators perform sea-use acceptance reviews according to the approval documents for sea-use rights, the Law of the People's Republic of China on the Administration of the Use of Sea Areas, the Regulation on Sea-Use Rights, the Specifications for Sea Cadastral Surveys, and other relevant documents, laws, regulations, and technical specifications.

Sea-use acceptance involves the following major steps: (1) application for sea-use acceptance of the coastal reclamation project has been completed, (2) preliminary review of the application materials, (3) survey of the sea-use area of the completed coastal reclamation project, (4) issuance of the notice of sea-use acceptance, (5) on-site inspection, and (6) holding of a sea-use acceptance meeting. Figure 8.1 presents the working procedure for sea-use acceptance of a coastal reclamation project has been completed.

8.1.1 *Applying Sea-Use Acceptance for a Project has been Completed*

Within the 30 days following completion of a coastal reclamation project, the sea-use rights holder should apply to the ocean administrator who approved the reclamation project. This means the sea-use rights holder should apply to the ocean administrator who approved the reclamation project for the sea-use acceptance organization when the project has

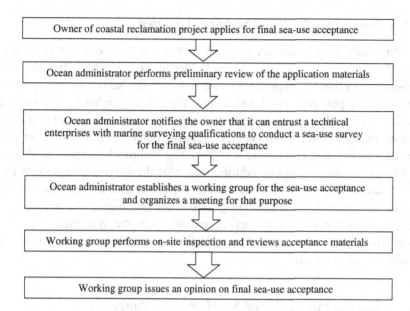

Figure 8.1 Working procedure for sea-use acceptance of a coastal reclamation project has been completed.

been completed. Materials to be submitted for the application include: (1) an application for sea-use acceptance of the project has been completed, (2) a sea-use dynamic monitoring report of a coastal reclamation project, (3) a design, construction, and supervision report of the coastal reclamation project, (4) a layout plan for the works to be constructed after completion, (5) copies of the sea-use rights certificate for the project and the royalty payment voucher, (6) a report on the implementation of stakeholder solutions, and (7) other documents and materials to be provided.

8.1.2 *Preliminary Review of the Application Materials*

The organizing ocean administrators of the sea-use acceptance should perform a preliminary review of the application materials submitted by the sea-use rights holder to determine their completeness and compliance with the relevant technical requirements. The organizing ocean administrators should notify the sea-use rights holder in a timely manner of any non-compliance identified, for which corrective measures should be taken by the sea-use rights holder.

8.1.3 *Surveying the Sea-Use to be Accepted*

If non-compliance issues are identified, the organizing ocean administrators should notify the sea-use rights holder in writing within five days of sea-use accepting the application materials that the survey for acceptance can begin. Upon receipt of the notice, the sea-use rights holder should entrust technical enterprises acceptable to the organizing ocean administrators and with marine-surveying qualifications to conduct an on-site sea-use survey and to prepare a report. The technical enterprises should notify the organizing ocean administrators of the survey time so that the latter can send an official to the site to supervise and witness the survey to ensure its accuracy. Whenever possible, the organizing ocean administrators should assign a surveying expert with the provincial sea-use dynamic supervision center to verify the coordinates of major vertices along the property line.

8.1.4 *Issuing the Notice of Sea-Use Acceptance*

After the on-site sea-use survey, the sea-use rights holder should submit the report prepared by the technical enterprises to the organizing ocean administrators. The latter should review the report and issue the notice of sea-use acceptance if the review flags no technical issues in the report. To review the sea use in more detail, some organizing ocean administrators require an additional review step to be taken by ocean administrators at the county or city level. In such cases, the ocean administrators at that level have to review the materials and verify their on-site sea-use surveying. They should then issue the review opinions for qualified application materials and report the opinions to the province-level ocean administrators.

8.1.5 *On-Site Inspection*

The organizing ocean administrators should establish a working group on sea-use acceptance, composed of officials with the local ocean, land, water conservation, and environmental protection authorities at the province level (or that of the autonomous region/municipality directly under the central government) and at the city (county) level, as well as survey experts who have no vested interest in the coastal reclamation project. The main tasks of the sea-use acceptance working group include:

(1) reviewing the survey report submitted by the on-site survey enterprises, (2) reviewing the sea-use dynamic monitoring report of the coastal reclamation project, (3) checking compliance with national and industrial technical standards (specifications), and (4) taking actions against or proposing solutions for the major issues identified in the final sea-use acceptance. The working group conducts the process of sea-use acceptance through on-site inspections; briefings from the sea-use rights holder and responsible for construction, design, supervision, the sea-use acceptance survey, and sea-use dynamic monitoring; inquiries; and requests for access to data. It forms its opinions through sea-use acceptance research. Those opinions must be signed and sealed by the sea-use acceptance group leader (Minqiang Tang *et al.*, 2009).

Since the implementation of the Sea-Use Acceptance Management for Sea-Area Use after Completion regulation in 2007, ocean administrators at various levels nationwide have organized the sea-use acceptance for more than 800 coastal reclamation projects. Efforts in this regard have effectively improved the sea-use acceptance and supervision of coastal reclamation projects. However, as the number of coastal reclamation projects to be accepted keeps increasing, we expect that there will be more issues in implementing regulations and in reviewing and managing the final sea-use acceptance of coastal reclamation projects.

8.2 Survey Techniques for Final Sea-Use Acceptance of Coastal Reclamation Projects

The survey for the final sea-use acceptance includes the definition and survey of the property line and calculating the sea-use area of the coastal reclamation project. The definition and survey of the property line have specific rules for general projects, "inland" projects, and areas of reclaimed land. The calculating sea-use area for the final sea-use acceptance also involves calculated measured area and confirmation of the actual sea-use area.

8.2.1 *Definition and Survey of the Property Line for the Final Sea-Use Acceptance of Coastal Reclamation Projects*

(1) *Definition and survey of the property line for general projects*: In the Specifications for the Sea Cadastral Surveys, the sea-use boundary for

"land reclamation projects" is defined as follows: "The inner property line is the original shoreline or the line connecting artificial shores. The outer and side property lines are the outer edges of bases of cofferdams, embankments, and backfilled materials under the water (toe lines)." For protection against tidal floods and waves, most coastal reclamation projects involve the building of revetments, which can be generally classified as vertical, stepped, or sloped. For projects with vertical revetments, the top and toe lines are on the same vertical plane. When surveying for final sea-use acceptance, the inner property lines are generally the original shorelines as designated in the approval of the coastal reclamation project. For surveys conducted after 2008, the shorelines are generally determined as per the statutory shoreline data. The outer and side property lines are the top lines of the revetments, which are usually measured with RTK technology. With the property boundary defined by the inner, outer, and side property lines, it is possible to calculate the actual sea-use area of a coastal reclamation project (see Figure 8.2).

For projects with stepped or sloped revetments, as the top and toe lines are not on the same vertical surface, the outer and side property lines are the toe lines of the revetments underwater. At the time of the survey for sea-use acceptance, the toe lines of the sloped revetments underwater are surveyed with a side scan sonar, which can generate clear slope reflection images. Together with the construction design data of the project, they can be used to determined reasonably and accurately the location of the toe line or the outer boundary of the area of land reclamation (see Figure 8.3).

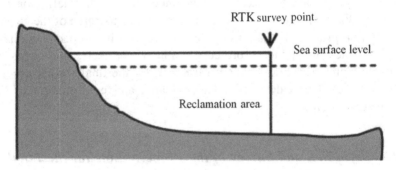

Figure 8.2 Definition and survey of the property lines for projects with vertical revetments.

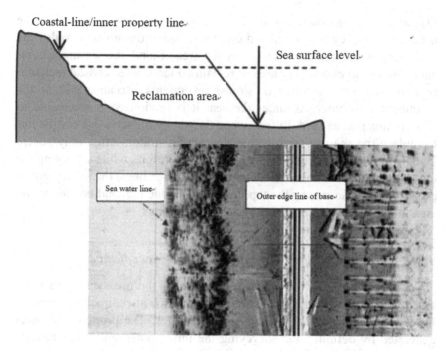

Figure 8.3 Definition and survey of the property lines for projects with sloped revetments.

(2) *Definition and survey of the property line for "inland" projects*: For "inland" projects within a regional sea-use plan for construction projects, because the boundary defined in the original approval document has been occupied by other, completed coastal reclamation projects, the traditional survey method is no longer applicable. In this case, the original shoreline approved in the project approval is used as the inner boundary. The outer and side property lines should be the lines set out by the construction enterprises along the property corners approved for defining the property line, which should be checked by the survey enterprises for confirmation. Upon confirmation, the location and area of the coastal reclamation can be deemed to be in compliance with the approval requirements. That is, the approved property corners are used as the measured points for sea-use acceptance. Normally, the allowed difference between the points used by the construction enterprises and the verified points is 5.0 cm.

(3) *Definition and survey of the area of reclaimed land*: As the sea-use acceptance survey for completed coastal reclamation projects is also the basis for land administrators to ratify the area of land, the sea-use acceptance also involves a survey area of reclaimed land. Most coastal reclamation projects have stepped or sloped revetments. Because part of the revetment is submerged under the sea, it is obviously unacceptable to classify this part as land. In fact, when they issue the land-use certificates to replace the sea-use certificates, land administrators often only accept land up to the area defined by the top lines. Therefore, while surveying the toe lines of the revetments to determine the outer lines, the survey enterprises should also survey the top lines and include the land boundary and area in the survey report and the attached drawings.

8.2.2 Calculation Area for Final Sea-Use Acceptance

(1) *Calculation measured area*: Calculation of the measured area is an essential part of analyzing the survey data, which also directly determine the land area shown in the land-use certificates. The property line data generated by defining and surveying the inner, outer, and side property lines can be combined to define a closed sea-use unit and generate complete boundary information for a specific project. As shown in the following equations, the area S can be calculated manually or with a computer graphics processing system by employing a coordinate analysis method according to the plane rectangular coordinates for each property corner x_i, y_i, where i is the serial number of a point.

$$S = \frac{1}{2}\left[x_1\left(y_2 - y_n\right) + x_2\left(y_3 - y_1\right) + \cdots + x_{n-1}\left(y_n - y_{n-2}\right) + x_n\left(y_1 - y_{n-1}\right)\right]$$

or

$$S = \frac{1}{2}\left[y_1\left(x_2 - x_n\right) + y_2\left(x_3 - x_1\right) + \cdots + y_{n-1}\left(x_n - x_{n-2}\right) + y_n\left(x_1 - x_{n-1}\right)\right]$$

$$(8.1)$$

In the calculation of actual area, the side scan sonar system may identify hundreds of property corners, the coordinates of which will be used in the calculation of the area. Nevertheless, in recording and presenting, for the sake of simplicity, the number of coordinate points will be reduced as long as the area remains unchanged. For example, the drawing of actual property lines is prepared with the coordinates of the reduced points for presenting information such as the user of the sea area, the approved area of land reclamation, the actual area of land reclamation, the coordinates of the actual property corners (inner and outer property corners), the coordinate system and projection parameters, the survey unit, survey qualifications, and the drawer and reviewer of the drawing.

At present, the generally sea-use accepted calculation method for a measured area is "measured area = approved area + over-reclaimed area – un-reclaimed area." That is, the measured area is determined by the "approved area," "over-reclaimed area," and "un-reclaimed area," and any error in these will cause a deviation in the calculation results of the measured area. The term "over-reclaimed area" refers to the area enclosed by the approved property line and the measured property line beyond the property line. The term "un-reclaimed area" refers to the area enclosed by the approved property line and the measured property line within the property line. In calculating the over-reclaimed area and the un-reclaimed area, the surveying unit needs to compare the measured and the approved property lines. Therefore, in order to ensure the consistency of the data, it seems to be a good choice to calculate the measured area by using the calculated area enclosed by the approved boundary. However, if there is a difference between the approved area and the calculated area in the certificate of sea-use rights, accuracy in the calculation measured area will be affected. In such cases, if the approved area on the certificate of sea-use rights is used for the calculation, the measured area is bound to be inconsistent with the area enclosed by the measured property corners. In addition, since the area data for a marine parcel are recorded to the fourth decimal place in units of hm^2, that is, the accuracy is 1.0 m^2. Thus, in calculating the over-reclaimed and un-reclaimed area, the rounding of the figures may also introduce some errors into the calculated area.

(2) *Confirmation of the actual sea-use area for coastal reclamation projects*: The sea-use acceptance survey aims to confirm consistency between the location and area as built and the location and area as approved. Specifically, it involves surveying the boundary as built and then comparing the measured area and the approved area. In the calculation area for final sea-use acceptance, there is usually a discrepancy between the

calculated area and the approved area. The discrepancy can be explained by the following three reasons.

First, the difference in the area may be caused by a discrepancy between the coordinate system or projection zone of the approved original property corners and the coordinate system or projection zone adopted for sea-use acceptance mapping. The conversion between geodetic coordinates and plane coordinates is also an important cause of accuracy loss. In addition, the decimal place to which the measurement is recorded for coordinates of approved property corners also affects accuracy, which is related to area error. In China, when the relevant technical specifications and documents have not been issued and a unified surveying datum has not been adopted for sea-use management, the sea area approved might adopt different coordinate systems (mainly the 1954 Beijing coordinate system) and projection zones (mainly the 3-degree zone), with the values for geodetic coordinates being recorded to different decimal places. By contrast, the Specifications for Sea Cadastral Surveys require that the World Geodetic System of 1984 (WGS-84) and the 0.5-degree zone be adopted. Due to the improvement of measurement accuracy, the errors for land operations are in centimeters. For sea-use surveys, the values for coordinates of property corners are recorded to the third decimal place. Discrepancies in the area are very common and classified as an unavoidable error. Nevertheless, considering the minimal area difference, the area originally approved is usually used to verify the area.

Second, for some coastal reclamation projects that have an arc boundary, the area approved in the certificate of sea-use rights is calculated according to the boundary. However, in the coordinate table of property corners for the certificate, only the vertices are used as the property corners, without marking the coordinates of the circle center and radian for the arc. In verifying the approved area, the surveying unit might only calculate the area for the parcel enclosed by the lines that connect the property corners on the certificate of sea-use rights. Therefore, a considerable difference is inevitable because the calculated area is that of a polygon rather than of a shape with an arc boundary. In an area comparison analysis, the conversion of the arc property line to a polygonal line also makes it difficult to verify the over-reclaimed and un-reclaimed areas. If the original approved area is used as the verified area, the results obtained would be inconsistent with those derived by using a calculation method that takes into account the area of the over-reclaimed and un-reclaimed parts or by introducing errors in the verified area. On the other hand, the results derived by calculating the area of the polygon would be even more inappropriate. Therefore, for such projects, marking the mathematical parameters of an arc property line is recommended on the certificate of sea-use rights.

Third, a large difference may arise between the approved area and the verified one from calculation mistakes. These might be caused by mistakes made in completing the certificate of sea-use rights. It is necessary to double-check the coordinates of the property corners for accuracy. The confirmed mistakes in an approved area should be passed up to a relevant authority for recalculation. The royalty for the sea area would need to be adjusted retrospectively according to the area recalculated and confirmed.

8.3 Techniques for Final Sea-Use Acceptance of Coastal Reclamation Projects

The sea-use acceptance survey is demanding in terms of accuracy, which must be assured through several technical measures, such as the selection of appropriate survey instruments, control over the accuracy, the compilation of marine parcel maps, and area calculation. This section will focus on discussing the selection of surveying instruments, control over the accuracy, and the compilation of marine parcel maps.

8.3.1 *Survey Instruments Used in the Final Sea-Use Acceptance of Coastal Reclamation Projects*

The main instruments used in sea cadastral surveys are the rangefinder, theodolite, total station theodolite, and differential global positioning system (DGPS). Given the need for an accurate area, which is the basis of the issuance of the certificate of land-use rights, accuracy requirements should be strict. Since most of the reclamation projects in China are carried out in the coastal zone, the widely used measuring instruments are the radio beacon-differential global position system (RBN-DGPS) and receiver combination or the RTK GPS receiver. The RBN-DGPS combination incorporates a GPS satellite positioning system and a beacon system. The GPS station performs a real-time calculation of the difference in satellite pseudorange (the difference between the GPS pseudorange and the known pseudorange). The correction signal generated by the beacon system's feature of signal modulation and broadcasting is broadcast in real time and continuously within an effective range. GPS mobile devices can process the signal received and add the correction value to the result generated by the GPS device itself to improve positioning accuracy. The RTK technology enables the real-time processing of the difference between the carrier phases observed in two stations. That is, the carrier phase collected by the reference station is transmitted to the receiver to determine the coordinates by calculating the difference. Positioning accuracy can reach the centimeter level. This technology is widely used in fields requiring high-accuracy dynamic positioning.

The side scan sonar is used mostly to determine the position of the toe line of a revetment by generating clear slope reflection images on an acoustic imaging device. Take the EdgeTech 4,200 side scan sonar as an example. When it is set to operate at a range of 400 kHz and 100 m, the resolution along the track for the image is 2 cm. When the range is set to 25 m or 50 m, the resolution can be finer. In terms of accuracy, the resolution of side scan sonar images is comparable to that of an RTK positioning device. In side scan sonars, the resolution is mainly determined by the technical means for post data processing. An ordinary side scan sonar system requires the measurement of paper charts to acquire the coordinate data of the target, and consequently, accuracy cannot be guaranteed. With a more accurate digital processing flow, any issues with the precision of the tow fish position and determination of the target position can be solved. First, the layback can be calibrated according to the consistency of the target in two surveys carried out in uniform velocity and in opposite directions. For the final acceptance of coastal reclamation projects, with a generally short towing cable—as short as 3.0–5.0 m—the calibration can correct the layback error perfectly. Any error due to underwater sound speed should then be compensated for because side scan sonar determines the distance on both sides through acoustic waves. Given the difference between the sound speed of 1,500 m/s and 1,530 m/s, a distance error of 2% would arise. That is, at the range scale of 25 m, the positioning error could reach 0.5 m. Therefore, for high resolution, compensation for the sound speed error is indispensable. Sound speed error could be compensated for completely in this way. In addition to the correction of layback and sound speed errors, employing professional post-processing software for side scan sonar is also necessary. The software could process data digitally, eliminating the error caused by manual operation using paper charts.

8.3.2 *Accuracy Requirements for Final Sea-Use Acceptance Surveys of Coastal Reclamation Projects*

According to the Specifications for Sea Cadastral Surveys and Specifications for Surveying Areas of Sea Use, the accuracy requirements for surveys are as follows: "The position error of the plane control point for sea cadastral surveys should not exceed ±5 cm. Accuracy for property corners: for property corners or marking points on the artificial shoreline, structures, and other fixed markers, the measurement accuracy should be better than 0.10 m; for other property corners or marking points on the marine parcel maps, the accuracy should be better than ±1.0 m, ± 3.0 m, and ±5.0 m for sea areas within 20 km, 20–50 km, and over 50 km from the shore, respectively." Since the artificial shore will be formed after the completion of coastal reclamation projects, the measurement accuracy for property corners for the final sea-use acceptance of projects should be better than 0.10 m.

For some projects, RBN-DGPS is used to survey the land edge of the reclaimed area. Within the coverage range of the RBN-DGPS, the sub-meter GPS receiver can only achieve an accuracy better than two root mean squares (at a confidence level of 95%) for differential positioning. Therefore, the accuracy of the RBN-DGPS is inadequate for the requirements of the final sea-use acceptance survey for coastal reclamation projects. In practice, such poor accuracy would result in considerable area errors. Indeed, sea users often lodge objections to the measurement results of sea-use areas. With the application of survey technologies such as RTK GPS with a single reference station or a network RTK GPS continuously operating reference station (CORS), it is possible to obtain high-precision measurements of the property corners quickly and conveniently. Therefore, survey instruments such as single reference station RTK GPS, network RTK GPS (CORS), total station theodolites, and other measuring instruments should be used where possible for the final acceptance survey of coastal reclamation projects.

8.3.3 Methods for Compiling Marine Parcel Maps for Final Sea-Use Acceptance of Coastal Reclamation Projects

A marine parcel is a unit of sea area enclosed by the property line with defined spatial position, uses, and ownership. The marine parcel map is the sea cadastral map for the marine parcel, indicating the actual spatial location of the parcel, the property corners (their coordinates), property line, area, uses, ownership, and the relationships with adjacent marine parcels. Because the map is attached to the certificate of sea-use rights and the parcel file, which have been recognized legally in registering sea use, it can serve as legal evidence for the sea-area user to settle disputes on sea-area ownership.

(1) *The main contents of the marine parcel map*: The marine parcel map is built on the latest topographical map, nautical chart, or remote sensing imagery with the appropriate accuracy. The topographical information and features will be included to the extent that they are needed to present basic information about the marine parcel. Specifically, a marine parcel map comprises the following elements:

(a) *Mathematical elements*: These represent the basic mathematical information of the map, including projection, scale, control points, coordinate system, and elevation data. They also determine the coverage and location of the map and provide the basis for controlling other contents, ensuring that the map presents position, elevation, length, and area accurately.

(b) *Geographical elements*: These represent the natural and social phenomena related to geographical locations and distribution. They can be further classified into natural elements (such as those related to hydrology, topography, and biology) and social elements (such as administrative boundaries, roads, and population distribution).

(c) *Finishing elements*: These mainly refer to contents of the map that are included to facilitate reading and using, such as the drawing name, number, legend, map data description, and various words and figures used in the map.

The property line map for a marine parcel used by the coastal reclamation project represents a detailed layout of the project, the marine parcel's shape, the distribution of the property corners, the ownership scope, and the location relative to adjacent marine parcels. Specifically, the property line map comprises the following main contents.

(i) Information related to the property line, including the polygons, property lines, and property corners for the marine parcel and the units within it. The property corners are numbered with Arabic numerals from 1 in a counterclockwise direction. The graphic patterns for different sea uses of the internal polygons should be distinguishable.

(ii) The adjacent marine parcels, including their polygons, property lines, property corners, and project name (including the individual or organizational owners' names).

(iii) Relevant elements to reflect information about adjacent land and sea areas (including shoreline, isobathic lines, place names, obvious markers), relevant sea plans, or existing facilities and structures in the adjacent sea areas.

(iv) List of property corners in sequence, including their serial numbers and list of coordinates. The geodetic coordinates should be used and presented in degree, minute, and second to two decimal places after the second. The serial number of the property corners should be consistent with that on the map.

(v) List of internal units, property lines, and areas in the marine parcel. The internal units should be named according to the specific sea uses. The property line is represented by the property corners on the line connected by "—", and the beginning and the end property corners should be identical. The area should be presented in hm^2 and recorded to the fourth decimal place. The internal units' names should be consistent with those in "Record Form for Marine Parcel and Its Internal Units."

(vi) Other information, such as drawing name, coordinate system, scale, projection parameters, direction, drawing date, surveying unit, drawing unit, surveyor, compiler, and reviewer. The scale for the map could be set at 1:5,000 or larger so that the shape and distribution of the property corners are presented clearly.

For complex sea uses or uses that cover a large sea area, the map can be compiled using several sheets to represent the shape and distribution of the property corners simultaneously. One of the sheets can be used to represent the overall layout, while each zoomed part can be displayed on a separate sheet.

(2) *The method for compiling the marine parcel map*: The marine parcel map is compiled with high geometric accuracy to represent the boundary, characteristics in distribution, and relevant ownerships. As an important part of sea-use management, the compilation of the marine parcel map must meet two requirements. First, the map should be compiled with clear property lines, accurate coordinates, a precise area, well-defined boundaries in four directions, correct and complete notes, and appropriate scale. Second, the units or individuals responsible for the compilation of the marine parcel map should have qualifications for marine surveying and mapping (Katrine Soma and Arild Vatn, 2009).

As indicated by the name, the map is compiled for a marine parcel to indicate the use rights for an independent, homogeneous, and closed sea area. For two independent and closed sea areas of different types under the same project, separate marine parcel maps should be compiled. The compilation is entirely dependent on the analytical coordinates of all the property corners. The job is performed by a computer drawing system, such as AutoCAD, Arc-Map, or Arc-GIS. The compiled map should represent the following information accurately.

(a) *Property corners*: (i) The selection and definition of property corners should be in line with the requirements of the Specifications for Sea Cadastral Surveys (HY/T124-2009); (ii) the mapping of property corners should be based on the analytic coordinates and carried out by a computer drawing system; (iii) the property corners should be indicated by black dots; and (iv) the property corners are to be numbered counterclockwise successively from 1. The property corners for works and structures on the project site should be numbered first, while others on open water should be numbered later.

(b) *Property line*: (i) A closed property line can be formed by connecting the property corners for a marine parcel and its internal units in a counterclockwise direction successively. The enclosed area should be able to reflect the attributes and plane characteristics of the sea area; (ii) the mapping of the property line should be based on the analytic coordinates and carried out using a computer drawing system; (iii) the line should be drawn with a red solid line; and (iv) the markings on the property line map should indicate accurately the length of property line sections, as well as a safety distance from different sea-use attributes and structures.

(c) *The surface of a marine parcel*: The surface should be filled using different colors for different sea uses.

(d) *Assessment of area*: The area of the sea used by a project is the basis for approving the marine parcel map and sea-area ownership. The calculation of the area of the sea used should be comprehensive, accurate, and performed as per the following methods. First, the area of the sea used should be calculated separately for different sea uses. Second, the area of a marine parcel should be calculated according to the analytical method. When it is possible to acquire the x, y coordinates for each property corner in meters, the formula $S = 1/2\Sigma[x(y_i - y_j)]$ can be used, where S is the area of the marine parcel in m^2 and x_i and y_i are the horizontal and vertical coordinates for the ith property corner in meters. For marine parcels far away from the shoreline, since it is impossible to obtain the x, y coordinates for each of the property corners in meters, the area of the marine parcel can be calculated after conversion of the longitude and latitude coordinates of the property corners observed with a GPS device. Third, the sea area of the project is calculated in square meters, and the result is recorded without a decimal place; the results in hectares are recorded to the fourth decimal place. Fourth, for land reclamation projects and those with sloped structures, the area of the sea used and the reclaimed land for each of the sea-use units should be calculated separately.

(3) *Technical process for compiling the marine parcel map*:

(a) *Data collection and processing*: When preparing basic data and materials for compiling the map, the data to be collected include those on the current status of the marine parcel or the final design, the ownership and boundaries of adjacent marine parcels, basic geographical data about the sea area where the project is located, and the latest remote sensing imagery. Specifically, it is necessary, first, to select the data format suitable for mapping software. In cases where there are several data formats, they should be converted into one suitable format. Second, the CGCS 2000 coordinate system is currently required to compile the marine parcel map. Spatial data that are not in CGCS 2000 should be converted into the CGCS 2000 coordinate system. Third, the coverage of the data should be such that when the property is placed at the center of the map, the surrounding elements of the sea area are evenly distributed.

(b) *Determining the category and uses of the sea*: The uses of the sea in a marine parcel are determined according to relevant provisions on the classification of the uses and the first and second levels of classification.

(c) *Determining the coverage of the property line*: The steps involved include surveying the property corners of the marine parcel accurately, processing and reading the data for each property corner, connecting the points for plotting the property line, considering the attributes of the property line of adjacent marine parcels, and determining the plane coverage of the property line according to the outermost boundary of all sea uses.

(d) *Compiling the location map for the marine parcel*: With regard to the geographical position of the marine parcel, the area covered by the property line of the marine parcel can be displayed as a pattern plot to indicate the geographical position and the relative position in terms of important geographical information.

(e) *Dividing the marine parcel into several internal units and calculating their areas*: A marine parcel can be divided into different units according to the areas covered by different sea uses. The areas for the same use that are separated from each other should be divided into different sea-use units. The areas of the units should be calculated separately.

(f) *Compiling the property line map for the marine parcel*: This involves presenting the shape of the marine parcel, layout of internal units, distribution of property corners, coverage of the property line, and location of adjacent marine parcels. The polygons for the internal units should be filled for different uses separately. The list of coordinates of the property corners, internal units, property lines, and areas should also be included.

(g) *Finish the drawing*: After completing the location map and property line map, the frame, mesh, and text should be added. The text should present the following information: projection, coordinate system, central longitude, elevation data, coordinate unit, scale, drawing unit, and compiler. The layout for the list of property corners, list of internal units, legend, scale, list of coordinate projection information, list of drawing units and compilers, and other information should be provided as appropriate. The drawings should be finished to ensure that they are neat, polished, and concise.

(h) *Quality checking*: Quality checking covers the completeness of the elements and contents, symbols used, color, conformity to the forms, and accuracy of drawing.
(i) *Output drawings*: AutoCAD can be used to output files in BMP format, and Arc-GIS can be used for JPG format. If drawings with a higher resolution and better printing quality are needed, drawing software can be used to print directly.

Chapter 9

Post Evaluation Methods for Coastal Reclamation Projects

9.1 Overview of Post Evaluation of Coastal Reclamation Projects

Post evaluation of coastal reclamation projects involves several tasks. The first is to observe the social and economic benefits offered and the ecological environmental impact caused by the projects over a certain period after they have been completed and put into operation. The second is to compare the observed results with those predicted by the Sea-Use Demonstration Report to identify the differences, on the basis of which it is possible to judge whether the predicted results are reasonable. In addition, a comprehensive evaluation of the observed social benefits, economic benefits, and ecological environmental impact can present a full picture of the actual impact of a project on the sea area and the effectiveness of compensation measures. The accuracy and rationality analysis of a series of predictions and decisions made before project implementation can pin down the reasons for any problematic and inaccurate predictions. Consequently, the analysis may not only improve the decision-making capacity of relevant enterprises and ocean administrators but also provide valuable inputs into enhancing construction project management, environmental protection management, economic management, and social management (Academic Divisions of Chinese Academy of Sciences, 2011). In other words, the post evaluation of coastal reclamation projects not only provides a technical means to improve the rational use of invested funds, investment gains, and sea management, and related decision-making but also offers valuable inputs for developing relevant policies. To sum up, the post evaluation is a comprehensive exercise. It analyses and evaluates the social, economic, and environmental impact and externalities of coastal reclamation projects after they have been put into operation. The objectives are to identify issues, understand reasons, learn from experiences and lessons, and propose countermeasures and recommendations, and then to enhance project management and improve overall benefits in terms of the economy, society, and the environment. Therefore, post evaluation can be regarded as a follow-up to sea-use demonstration. It can help to preserve the fragile ecological environment in coastal zones effectively. In implementing sustainable development of the marine economy, post evaluation is indispensable in that it is a useful tool for safeguarding sustainable development (Shuguang Wang *et al.*, 2008).

9.1.1 *Objectives of the Post Evaluation*

(1) *To verify the results predicted in the sea-use demonstration report*: The results predicted in the sea-use demonstration report are based on research, analysis, and predictions made before implementing coastal reclamation projects. The appropriateness of the project decision-making, soundness of the prediction approaches, correctness in applying mathematical and physical models, and accuracy of the conclusions and predictions have to be verified when the projects are put into operation (Guochang Wang *et al.*, 1999). Through the post evaluation, it is possible to verify the appropriateness of the evaluation approaches adopted in the sea-use demonstration and the accuracy of the evaluation conclusions by comparing the results predicted in the demonstration report and those observed, in terms of social benefits, economic benefits, and environmental impact after the projects are implemented.

(2) *To provide valuable inputs to enhance management of coastal reclamation*: Any social benefits, economic benefits, and environmental impact will emerge within a certain period after coastal reclamation projects are completed and put into operation. By investigating the changes produced by coastal reclamation projects on the society, economy, and environment, the post evaluation can detect any trends in the changes, identify favorable and unfavorable factors, and propose measures for increasing the favorable effects and reducing the unfavorable effects, thereby providing valuable inputs to enhance the management of coastal reclamation.

(3) *To set an example for project design and post evaluation of coastal reclamation projects in other regions*: Coastal reclamation projects are marine development activities that generally involve sizable investments; high-risk, large-scale, broad impacts; and numerous other factors. It is difficult to predict and evaluate their social contribution, economic benefits, and environmental impact. In China, post evaluation of coastal reclamation projects is only a recent endeavor, with relevant theories and approaches that still need to be improved, and many aspects of the evaluation are hard to quantify. Nevertheless, the post evaluation provides an opportunity to summarize successful experiences and valuable lessons from projects—in terms of technology, the economy, the environment, and management—to explore the theories and methods of evaluation in the sea-use demonstration and to make the prediction method more reasonable and the evaluation results more realistic. The sea-use demonstrations and project designs for similar projects could also learn from the results of previous post evaluations.

(4) *To inform the adjustment and optimization of the monitoring scheme*: In the design of the dynamic monitoring station network for coastal reclamation projects, the monitoring scheme is developed on the basis of original environmental conditions, predictions, and evaluations, which may be different from the actual conditions after the project has been put into operation. In cases where there are changes to the natural and social environmental conditions, the design of the station network needs to be tested against the new conditions. As mentioned before, the post evaluation involves systematic research on the social contributions, economic benefits, and environmental impact of the projects after they have been put to use, as well as a comprehensive understanding of the factors and a systematic analysis of the monitoring data. On the basis of the information, it is possible to adjust and optimize the monitoring scheme as appropriate.

(5) *To inform the approval of subsequent plans*: The post evaluation is also a comprehensive check of (a) compliance with initial planning in terms of the functional positioning, spatial distribution, and layout design of the project; (b) the intensive/frugal use of the sea area and the social and economic benefits of the implemented projects; and (c) the actual impact of the implemented projects on sensitive environmental targets and the treatment of stakeholders. A comprehensive analysis of the social,

economic, and environmental benefits of the implemented projects can inform ocean administrators' approval of future plans.

(6) *To promote a rational distribution of marine economic activities and enhance management of marine functional zoning*: The post evaluation of coastal reclamation projects needs to be integrated into the sea-use demonstration. It also should be an essential step in implementing the project and an essential part of the management system for the use of marine resources. It can effectively promote the healthy, stable, and sustainable development of the marine economy, continuously improve the structure of marine industries, and optimize the distribution of marine economic activities. In addition, it can strengthen the real impact of marine functional zoning, improve sea users' awareness of marine environmental protection, and develop public awareness of marine issues, thereby enabling the sustainable and sound development of China's marine industrial economy.

9.1.2 *Rationales for the Post Evaluation*

Developed countries such as the United States, Australia, and Japan pay great attention to the development and protection of marine resources. They have built sound legal frameworks for the development and conservation of marine resources. Indeed, they introduced the post evaluation system and integrated it into ocean management. Since the 1970s, the post evaluation of projects completed in these countries has always put environmental protection and environmental benefits ahead of economic and social benefits. A project without environmental benefits, particularly a project that may cause pollution to the marine environment, has no chance of being approved. It is unthinkable to gain short-term economic benefits at the cost of environmental damage. By contrast, the post evaluations of non-coastal reclamation projects completed in China in recent years have focused on social and economic benefits only, without due consideration for the environmental impact. China should learn from the aforementioned countries in the post evaluation of marine engineering projects to enhance its capacity in environmental protection and to realize the sustainable development of the maritime economy (Anning Suo *et al.*, 2012b). With the United Nations Convention on the Law of the Sea taking effect and the incoming "Ocean Century," China needs to strengthen its supervision and management of its sea-area environment and resources and their use and to implement post evaluations accordingly. These measures are critical to the targets of developing marine resources reasonably, preserving and improving the marine environment, and implementing the strategy of sustainable development to the fullest extent.

Since the founding of the People's Republic of China, China has carried out large-scale coastal reclamation activities, which have achieved remarkable social and economic outcomes and the rapid development of its marine economy. However, due to issues in the management of coastal reclamation projects, especially the lax regulation in dynamic monitoring of projects that have been built and put into operation, numerous adverse effects have been observed. Post evaluations could extend and improve sea-use demonstration and the evaluation of marine environmental impact. They re-evaluate coastal reclamation projects after they have been put into operation in terms of their benefits and impact. By learning from the experiences and lessons identified, they may enhance the decision-making capacity, management skills, and environmental, social, and economic benefits of future projects. They also enable the adequate supervision and management of the environmental, social, and economic impact of projects for the: (1) reasonable reservation and use of shoreline resources, (2) preservation and improvement of the shoreline environment, (3) expansion of space for productivity growth and enhancement of the potential for economic development, and (4) promotion of short- and long-term social and economic development.

Furthermore, post evaluations can also contribute to national targets of maintaining the sustainable development of the marine economy and building a conservation-oriented society. The Regulations on Prevention and Control of Pollution and Damages to the Marine Environment by Coastal Engineering Construction Projects, which took effect on November 1, 2006, also provided a certain legal basis for the implementation of post evaluations. Article 20 of the Regulations clearly states that should ocean engineering works have an environmental impact that is larger than permitted during its construction and operation, the construction enterprises must organize a post evaluation of the environmental impact within 20 working days of the date on which the limit was exceeded. Correction measures must be taken on the basis of the conclusions of the evaluation. The conclusions and the measures are to be filed with the initial ocean administrator that approved the Environmental Impact Report for the engineering works. The initial ocean administrator may also instruct the construction unit to implement a post evaluation and take corrective measures accordingly. As a maritime power, China still does not have a post evaluation system for coastal reclamation projects. It needs a long-term plan for the system by building on its experiences of evaluations.

Independent consultants with the appropriate skills should complete the post evaluation and the preparation of its report. Institutions, organizations, and relevant expert panels that participated in evaluation for the sea-use demonstration should be excluded. The qualifications of relevant institutions and organizations should be inspected and a new expert panel selected in order to ensure that the post evaluation is fair, objective, and sound.

9.2 Post Evaluation Methods for Marine Environmental Impact of Coastal Reclamation Projects

The impact of coastal reclamation on the marine environment is generally most noticeable in terms of the marine biological and ecological environment, marine hydrodynamics, erosion/siltation conditions, water quality, and sediment quality (Anning Suo *et al.*, 2012c). The marine biological and ecological environment matters most to the phytoplankton, zooplankton, shallow-sea benthic, intertidal, and nekton biological communities. The indicators chosen to gauge the impact include species composition (including the number of species and the ratio of the number of species in a particular community to the total number of species), dominant species (community), biomass, density, number of species, and diversity index. For marine hydrodynamic and erosion/siltation conditions, the available indicators mainly include flood current velocity, current direction, tidal range, tidal prime, and erosion/siltation depth and area. Water quality and sediment quality are measured mainly by analyzing and evaluating the concentration of several common pollutants.

9.2.1 *System of Indicators for the Post Evaluation of the Marine Environmental Impact of Coastal Reclamation Projects*

By profiling the impact of coastal reclamation projects on the marine environment, we have chosen four indicators—biomass density, number of biological species, biomass/primary productivity, and biodiversity index—for each of five biological communities: the phytoplankton, zooplankton, shallow-sea benthic, intertidal, and nekton biological communities. In total, there will be 20 evaluation indicators. For marine hydrodynamic and erosion/siltation conditions, the indicators used are the flood current velocity, ebb current velocity, spring tidal range, and spring tidal prime. The active phosphates, inorganic nitrogen, and petroleum-related indicators are used to evaluate water quality. In terms of sediment quality, one evaluation indicator is used (Anning Suo *et al.*, 2012d).

In the 1970s, Saaty T. L. developed the analytic hierarchy process (AHP), a quantifying approach for a comprehensive evaluation of multiple indicators in a hierarchical structure. When applying this approach, the user needs to allocate elements related to a decision problem to a hierarchical structure formed by the goal, criteria, and solutions. Then, a decision-making matrix can be constructed by judging the relative importance of each element by pairwise comparison of the elements on a specific level. This allows the options to be ranked in order of their relative importance. In recent years, AHP has been widely applied as an effective method for weight indicators. The post evaluation of the marine environmental impact of coastal reclamation projects involves multiple aspects, such as marine ecology, marine hydrodynamics, water quality, and sediment quality. Its goal covers indicators on several levels and in a complex structure. Common evaluation methods cannot help to define the interactions among the indicators and are more subjective. By contrast, by using the AHP method and assigning a weight to each of the levels, a final marine environmental impact score can be obtained. Thus, the AHP is useful for post evaluations.

According to the AHP's basic principles, the system of indicators for the post evaluation comprises the following levels: goal, criteria, factor, and indicator. The overall goal addressed by the post evaluation is defined as the marine environmental impact of coastal reclamation project A. The criteria level covers two parts: marine biology B1 and marine environment B2. The factor level covers eight parts: phytoplankton C1, zooplankton C2, benthic organisms C3, intertidal organisms C4, nekton C5, hydrodynamic conditions C6, water quality C7, and sediment quality C8. The indicator level includes 20 indicators for the marine biological communities, such as biomass density, number of biological species, biomass/primary productivity, and the biodiversity index. For marine hydrodynamic conditions, the indicators used include flood current velocity, ebb current velocity, spring tidal range, and spring tidal prime. The active phosphates, inorganic nitrogen, and petroleum-related indicators are used for water quality. In terms of sediment quality, one indicator related to sulfides is used. Thus, we have built a system of indicators for the post evaluation of the marine environmental impact of coastal reclamation projects, as shown in Figure 9.1.

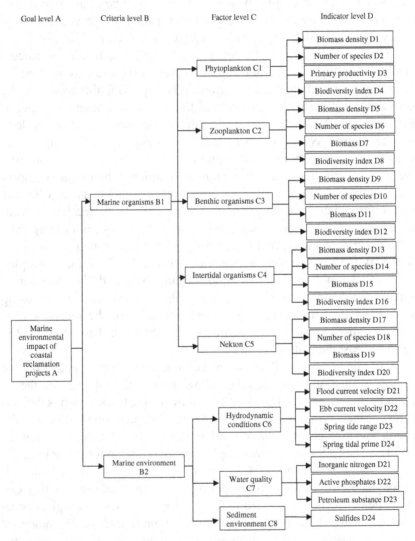

Figure 9.1 System of indicators for the post evaluation of the marine environmental impact of coastal reclamation projects.

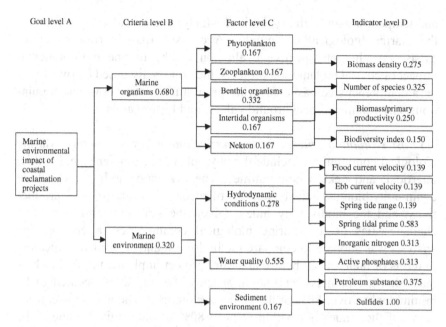

Figure 9.2 Weights of indicators for the post evaluation of the marine environmental impact of coastal reclamation projects.

The AHP can then be employed to weigh the indicators at different levels. Specifically, relevant experts are engaged to compare the factors pairwise on the same level in terms of relative importance by working on a decision-making matrix. The Saaty T. L. 9-point scale comes in handy to assign values to the grades of excellence or importance. By solving the maximum eigenvalue, the priority weights for the indicators at each of the levels can be calculated. The calculation results can then be tested for consistency. Figure 9.2 presents the weights obtained through the above process for the system of indicators.

9.2.2 Criteria for the Post Evaluation of the Marine Environmental Impact of Coastal Reclamation Projects

Appropriate evaluation indicators and criteria are critical to the success of the evaluation. Setting such evaluation criteria has always been challenging. The factors that need to be taken into account include the marine environmental conditions themselves, complex human value orientations, and temperature and salinity, both of which have considerable effects on the marine biological community. A one-size-fits-all criterion barely exists. For the retrospective evaluation of the marine environmental impact of coastal reclamation projects, the criteria discussed below are set on a comprehensive basis, covering prior studies, state laws and regulations, environmental background values, and historical data.

(1) *Post evaluation criteria for the marine biological community*: Marine biological communities include the phytoplankton, zooplankton, benthic, intertidal, and nekton communities. The evaluation indicators include community biomass density, number of species, biomass/primary productivity, and the biodiversity index. Given the structural and functional characteristics of the marine biological communities, a comparative analysis was adopted to compare the biological and ecological indicators in terms of their values before and after project implementation. For biomass density, biomass, and some species, the impact is deemed to be minimal when over 80% of the values are retained. The impact is considerable if the values are within 60% to 80% of the original values. The impact is enormous if the values are 60% of the original values. The criteria for biodiversity are set on the basis of studies on the relationship between the biodiversity index and pollution. A biodiversity index less than or equal to 1 indicates that the biological community is unstable due to the substantial ecological impact of coastal reclamation projects. An index greater than one and less than or equal to 3 indicates that the biological community is good, and the impact of the projects is limited. When the index is greater than 3, it indicates that the biological community is stable and that the impact is minimal or barely noticeable. The criteria for benthic biomass are set according to the *Technical Guidelines for Evaluating Ecological and Environmental Impact of Coastal Reclamation Projects,* according to which the impact of coastal reclamation projects on the benthic biological community is minimal when the benthic biomass is greater than or equal to 100 g/m^2.

When the biomass of benthic organisms is greater than 20 g/m^2 but less than 100 g/m^2, the projects have a substantial impact on the benthic biological community. When the biomass is less than or equal to 20 g/m^2, the projects have an enormous impact on the benthic biological community. The primary productivity of phytoplankton is evaluated against criteria based on the *Survey and Research on the Habitat Environment of*

Table 9.1   Criteria for post evaluation indicators of the marine environmental impact of coastal reclamation projects.

Indicator	Minimal impact	Considerable impact	Enormous impact
The diversity index of phytoplankton	>3	1–3	≤1
Biomass density index of phytoplankton	>80%	60–80%	≤60%
Number of phytoplankton species	>80%	60–80%	≤60%
Primary productivity (mgC/(m²·d))	≤200	200–300	>300
Biodiversity index of zooplankton	≤1	1–3	>3
Density index of zooplankton	>80%	60–80%	≤60%
Biomass index of zooplankton	>80%	60–80%	≤60%
Index of number of zooplankton species	>80%	60–80%	≤60%
Biomass of benthic organisms (g/m²)	≤20	20–100	>100
Biodiversity index of benthic organisms	≤1	1–3	>3
Index of number of benthic species	>80%	60–80%	≤60%
Density of benthic organisms	>80%	60–80%	≤60%
Biodiversity index of intertidal organisms	>80%	60–80%	≤60%
Density index of intertidal organisms	>80%	60–80%	≤60%
Index of number of species of intertidal organisms	>80%	60–80%	≤60%
Biomass index of intertidal organisms	>80%	60–80%	≤60%
Biodiversity index of nekton	>80%	60–80%	≤60%
Biomass index of nekton	>80%	60–80%	≤60%
Density index of nekton	>80%	60–80%	≤60%
Index of number of nekton species	>80%	60–80%	≤60%
Inorganic nitrogen content (μg/L)	>500	400–500	≤300
Active phosphates content (μg/L)	>45	30–45	≤30
Petroleum substances content (μg/L)	>50	10–50	≤10
Sulfide content (× 10⁻⁶)	>600	500–600	≤500
Flood current velocity index	>80%	60–80%	≤60%
Ebb current velocity index	>80%	60–80%	≤60%
Spring tide range index	>80%	60–80%	≤60%
Spring tidal prime index	>80%	60–80%	≤60%

Biological Resources, a national marine survey special project from 1997. When the primary productivity is less than or equal to 200 mgC/(m²·d), the coastal reclamation projects have minimal impact on primary productivity. When the primary productivity is greater than 200 mgC/(m²·d) but less than 300 mgC/(m²·d), the projects have a considerable impact on primary productivity. When the primary productivity is greater than 300 mgC/(m²·d), the projects have an enormous impact on primary productivity.

(2) *Evaluation criteria for water and sediment environment*: Factors for the water and sediment environment are evaluated against the criteria in *Marine Water Quality Standards* (GB3097—1997) and *Marine Sediment Quality* (GB18668—2002) and classified into three grades according to the results. The national Category II standard is used as a threshold to determine whether an impact qualifies as enormous. Table 9.1 summarizes the threshold values for the evaluation indicators.

To quantify the evaluation results, the values are assigned according to the following criteria: the value assigned is 1 for minimal impact, 2 for considerable impact, and 3 for enormous impact. The higher the value, the greater the impact of coastal reclamation activities on the marine environment.

9.3 Post Evaluation Methods for Social and Economic Benefits of Coastal Reclamation Projects

The post evaluation covers social benefits, economic benefits, and ecological sea use. The evaluation of social benefits addresses the jobs created by a project after it has been put into operation, the increase in income, and the improvement of infrastructure such as transportation, health care, education, and sanitation for the reclaimed land and surrounding areas. The economic benefits comprise the economic value of the reclaimed land, the gains in social and economic development realized by the construction and development of the coastal reclamation projects, the economic output of the reclaimed land, and any contribution to an increase in fiscal revenue. The evaluation of ecological sea use addresses the implementation of the marine ecological red line system, ecological compensation system, shore consolidation, and restoration projects, shore ecological construction, and sea-area management requirements and environmental protection measures set out in the sea-use project approval.

9.3.1 *Evaluation Methods for Social Benefits from the Implemented Coastal Reclamation Projects*

The social benefits from the implemented coastal reclamation projects include fiscal revenue increases, job creation, job income increases for the general public, and road coverage, vegetation land, and water system on the reclaimed land.

(1) *Contribution to fiscal revenue*: The rate of tax payments from coastal reclamation projects is calculated by dividing the annual tax payment of each project in the reclaimed zone with the area of reclaimed land, as shown in the equation as follows.

$$R = \frac{\sum_{i=1}^{n} Z_i}{S},$$
(9.1)

where R is the rate of tax payment, Z is the ith project's annual tax payment, and s is the area of the ith project.

In China, the general fiscal revenue of government at various levels mainly includes taxes, gains generated by state-owned assets (including profits, rents, dividends, bonuses, charges against fund users), government charges (comprising stipulated fees and royalties), special revenues (including an education surcharge and pollution levies), and other sources of revenue (including penalties and interests). Of these, tax is the most crucial source of revenue. Taxes can be further classified as goods and services taxes, income taxes, property taxes, and other taxes. For example, industrial enterprises are the main occupants of the reclaimed zone of the Yangpu Economic Development Zone. They generally need to pay income taxes for business operations, urban and rural construction taxes, and an education surcharge.

Enterprise income taxes are levied on income from business operations and other incomes of domestic enterprises and businesses. The taxes cover a wider range of taxpayers than the company income taxes do. The taxpayers of enterprise income taxes include all financially independent domestic enterprises or other organizations within the People's Republic of China. Specifically, these are:

(a) state-owned enterprises;
(b) collective enterprises;
(c) private enterprises;
(d) associated enterprises;
(e) joint-stock enterprises; and
(f) other organizations having income from production and business operations and other incomes.

The enterprise income taxes are levied against the income of the above taxpayers. They include income from the sale of goods, income from the provision of services, income from the transfer of property, income from dividends and bonuses, interest income, rental income, income from royalties, income from donations, and other incomes. According to the latest Income Tax Law, the statutory tax rate of 25% is applied consistently to both domestic and foreign enterprises. The tax rate for high-tech enterprises supported by China is 15%, that for small and low-profit enterprises is 20%, and that for non-resident enterprises is 20%.

Income tax payable by an enterprise = the tax rate applicable × current
taxable income
Taxable income = total amount of income − the deductible amount.

(2) *Coastal reclamation projects' contribution to job creation*: This contribution is represented by the employment index, which is calculated as employment income divided by the area of reclaimed land, as shown in the equation below.

$$JY = \frac{Q \times G}{A}, \tag{9.2}$$

where JY is the employment index, Q is the number of jobs created by the coastal reclamation projects, G is the average annual income of the employed population, and A denotes the area of reclaimed land.

The improvement of public infrastructure is represented by road coverage, which is calculated as the total length of the highway in the coastal reclamation zone divided by the zone's area.

9.3.2 Evaluation Methods for Economic Benefits of Coastal Reclamation Projects

(1) *Evaluation of the economic value of reclaimed land*: The most direct economic benefit of coastal reclamation comprises the land assets formed by the land increase from the reclamation. The reclaimed land provides essential space for the development of coastal and port industries. The economic value of the land can be evaluated according to the market price of the land resources for construction purposes. Specifically, the unit price of the land is determined according to the construction purpose, land grade, and current market price of comparable land. The land value can then be calculated by multiplying the unit price by the area of reclaimed land, as shown in the equation as follows:

$$P = P_0 \times S, \tag{9.3}$$

where P denotes the value of reclaimed land, P_0 is the average market price of land in the region, and S is the effective land area from coastal reclamation.

(2) *Gains in economic development realized by the construction and development of coastal reclamation projects*: Coastal reclamation projects can drive social and economic development through their investment in construction, procurement of materials, and infrastructure development, which are beneficial to regional economic growth. The gains can be estimated on the basis of the contribution rate of regional fixed asset investments to GDP growth in the region, as shown in the equation as follows:

$$R = W/\eta, \tag{9.4}$$

where R denotes the development gains, W is the fixed asset investment of a project, and η is the contribution rate of regional fixed asset investment to GDP growth.

At present, there are three main quantitative methods for measuring the contribution rate.

(a) *National income approach*:

(i) This method is based on the national income or expenditure approach for calculating GDP. The contribution to GDP by fixed asset investment is calculated by using the total fixed capital formation. It is calculated by determining the ratio of the increase in total fixed capital formation to the GDP increase for the same period. The ratio is defined as the contribution rate of fixed asset investment to economic growth. The extent to which fixed asset investment contributes to economic growth is often expressed as a percentage. The sum of the contribution rates of total fixed capital formation, final consumption, and net exports to economic growth calculated in this way should equal 100%.

(ii) Multiplying the contribution rate calculated in (i) as the weight by GDP growth over the evaluation period gives a percentage representing the contribution level of fixed asset investment to economic growth. The figure is usually expressed in terms of the percentage points of economic growth driven by fixed asset investments. The sum of the contribution levels of total fixed capital formation, final consumption, and net exports to economic growth calculated in this way should be equal to the GDP growth rate.

Fixed asset investment's contribution rate to economic growth =
$$\Delta I / \Delta \text{GDP} \times 100\%.$$
Fixed asset investment's contribution level to economic growth =
$$\Delta I / \Delta \text{GDP} \times (\Delta \text{GDP} / \Delta \text{GDP}_0) \times 100\%,$$

where ΔI denotes the increase in total fixed capital formation, ΔGDP is the increase in GDP in the evaluation period, ΔGDP_0 is the base period *GDP*, and $\Delta \text{GDP} / \Delta \text{GDP}_0$ is the growth rate of GDP over the evaluation period.

(b) *Investment multiplier method*: The investment multiplier is an essential concept in modern macroeconomics. Basically, it means that investment can lead to a GDP increase larger or several times larger than the investment. It is calculated as the output increase due to a unit increase in investment, as shown in the following equation:

GDP increase due to investment = investment multiplier × total fixed capital formation in the evaluation period
Investment multiplier = 1/(1–marginal propensity to consume).

(c) *Input–output analysis*: This method mainly uses an input-output table to represent the coefficient between input and output. It can be used to calculate the effect of a unit increase in the use of inputs in a sector or multiple sectors on sectoral output. These coefficients mainly reflect the status and role of a sector as determined by inter-sectoral technical and economic linkages in the national economy, so this method can only capture the impact of investment on the total output of each sector.

(3) *Evaluation of economic output of reclaimed land*: This evaluation covers the economic output of every development project that resides in the coastal reclamation zone, considering its industry type, production, market price, production cost, and business profits. The economic output is calculated as the sum of the annual economic output of every project in the reclaimed zone, as shown in the equation below:

$$Z = \sum_{i=1}^{10} p_i q_i,$$

(9.5)

where Z denotes the economic output of reclaimed land, p_i is the annual capacity of the ith project, q_i is the economic value of the unit capacity of the ith project, and i denotes the number of projects.

9.3.3 Evaluation Methods for Ecological Sea Use of Implemented Coastal Reclamation Projects

(1) *Evaluation of the implementation of the marine ecological red line in the use of sea areas*: This evaluation mainly involves a spatial overlay analysis for the reclamation zone and the marine ecological red line zone to define their relative positions (far from, adjacent to, partly breached, or completely breached). The evaluation also covers compliance with management requirements for the red line zone and whether the reclamation zone has a particular environmental impact on the red line zone. The analysis is mostly qualitative.

(2) *Evaluation of the implementation of ecological compensation measures in the use of sea areas*: This evaluation mainly deals with the implementation of the ecological compensation program, the means of compensation, and the use of compensation funds. It also covers shoreline ecological restoration, sea-area consolidation and restoration, and ecological system building in the sea area or along the shoreline. The evaluation is mostly a qualitative analysis, which is supplemented by the necessary quantitative evaluation.

(3) *Evaluation of implementing the management measures stipulated in the project approval for coastal reclamation projects*: This evaluation covers the implementation of measures for sea-use dynamic monitoring, marine environmental impact dynamic monitoring, environmental management, final acceptance, and establishment of the environmental threshold. Please refer to Section 7.3.

Chapter 10

Outlook of Coastal Reclamation Management in China

10.1 Background and Mandates of China's Coastal Reclamation Management

In the 21st century, for countries around the world, especially coastal countries, the ocean has increasingly become a valuable resource for boosting economic growth and entertaining innovative ideas for development. In a session of the 18th National Congress of the Communist Party, China introduced the critical strategy of becoming a maritime power and a beautiful country on the basis of its understanding of development trends and the international situation. President Xi Jinping and other state leaders attach great importance to the building of maritime power. They have mentioned the strategy on numerous occasions. In the 8th collective learning session of the Political Bureau, President Xi highlighted the importance of "promoting the development of maritime power by caring for, understanding, and managing the ocean." In recent years, coastal reclamation has been a powerful means of coastal development for China. It is critical to the development of an open port economy and the building of maritime power. At the same time, addressing the ecological and environmental issues caused by coastal reclamation activities and optimizing the spatial layout of reclamation projects would contribute to the goal of building a "beautiful China." Therefore, coastal reclamation management in China must implement the mandates of (1) controlling coastal reclamation activities strictly, (2) ensuring that coastal reclamation plays an active role in the development of the marine economy and building of maritime power, and (3) promoting innovations in the development of ecological civilization to address the issues caused by coastal reclamation activities as much as possible.

10.1.1 *Reclamation Management Should Ensure Development Space and Strategic Front for Maritime Power Building*

With accelerated migration of economic activities and production factors to the sea since the beginning of the 21st century, the population in large and megacities on the coast now accounts for 47.44% and 59.81% of the national total, respectively. With the implementation of the strategy of building maritime power, the next 10 years will be a critical period for China to extend its coastal industries, build coastal towns, and develop the marine economy. As more heavy industries, such as petrochemicals, steelmaking, shipbuilding, and nuclear power, migrate to coastal areas, the process of coastal town construction will maintain its full momentum. The huge demand for land resources in the industrialization and urbanization processes and China's strict rules for conserving the amount of arable land will create an enormous land supply gap in coastal areas. It is expected that during China's 13th Five-Year Plan period (2016–2020), the social and economic driving force behind the demand for coastal reclamation will still be substantial. From 2009 to 2011, the coastal reclamation activities in China used about 400 km of shoreline per year, and the annual natural shoreline loss is 120 km. The coastal reclamation projects have to extend from the high tidal flats to intertidal and sub-tidal zones as the sea areas available for reclamation shrank year by year. In the future, the development of the marine economy and coastal areas will face a severe shortage of sea space resources. Therefore, China needs to review the critical role of coastal reclamation in the implementation of its national marine development strategy, as well as the comprehensive adjustment and optimization of key major industries. With an objective understanding of the latest developments and emerging issues, China must then allocate the timings of sea-area development appropriately in line with its strategy of building maritime power, ensuring that it has the sea-area spatial resources needed for marine economic development and the construction of maritime power (Yuan Ren, and Wang Yongzhi, 2008).

10.1.2 *Coastal Reclamation Management Should Promote Ecological Civilization by Ensuring That Sea Uses Contribute to a "Beautiful China"*

The report to the 18th National Congress of the Communist Party of China proposed that "the building of an ecological civilization should be a task with high priority and integrated into all aspects and the overall process of economic, political, cultural, and social development, thereby building a beautiful China and achieving sustainable development for the Chinese nation." The ocean is an essential ecological barrier for the sustainable development of the coastal areas and even the whole country. The imbalance or destruction of the marine ecological environment not only directly affects the development of the marine economy and endangers the construction of a beautiful China but also indirectly endangers China's sustainable social and economic development. Coastal reclamation—an activity that completely changes the natural attributes of a sea area—should not be implemented without rigorous demonstration beforehand and strict management during the process. Otherwise, it will not only affect the rational development and sustainable utilization of sea areas but also may aggravate coastal erosion, resulting in sediment deposition in bays and ports, which would affect the flood discharge capacity of rivers and the shipping function of ports (Qi Wang and Tian Yingying, 2016). Because of their pollution, petroleum, steelmaking, chemical, shipbuilding, coal, and other industries with high energy consumption and substantial emissions place tremendous pressure on the marine environment when built on reclaimed land. Furthermore, they are vulnerable to marine disasters, such as typhoons and tsunami. In disastrous environmental emergencies, regional social and economic development could be endangered. Therefore, while meeting the demands of marine economic development for coastal reclamation, coastal reclamation management also needs to be innovative in order to minimize the impact of reclamation activities, exploring ways to build a beautiful China by using the sea in line with the principles of ecological civilization (Shuang Liu *et al.*, 2008).

10.2 Outlook for China's Practices of Coastal Reclamation Management

Coastal reclamation management is an essential dimension of sea-area management in China. With the demands of coastal social and economic development for shore space and the profound impact of coastal reclamation activities on the marine environment, coastal reclamation management will still be an important area of China's sea-area management over the next ten years. In the near future, ocean administrators and their technical support departments should focus on further improving China's technical framework for coastal reclamation management. With valuable inputs from experts in coastal reclamation management, the authors propose the following recommendations on the basis of a comprehensive review of China's practices in coastal reclamation management.

10.2.1 *Integration of the Concepts of Ecological Civilization into the Whole Process of Coastal Reclamation Management*

As mentioned earlier, building an ecological civilization is at the top of the agenda. Given the tightening constraints of sea-area spatial resources and a deteriorating marine ecological environment, it is essential to develop an ecological methodology for coastal reclamation management and to integrate the concepts of ecological civilization into the whole management process. First, with regard to marine zoning and planning, marine functional zoning, sea-area spatial planning theories, and the application of both must give due consideration to marine ecological systems. The restrictions on marine spatial uses must be imposed by giving top priority to ecological protection. No coastal reclamation activities should be allowed in non-ecologically sensitive sea areas. Second, the system of indicators for ecological evaluation for sea-use demonstration and marine environmental impact evaluation must be designed to preserve the service functions of marine ecological systems. The indicators must be able to capture the impact of coastal reclamation projects on marine ecological systems accurately. Third, the system of indicators for supervising coastal reclamation activities should be complete, easy to operate, accurate, and efficient in order to preserve the marine ecological environment and its ecological systems (Jinzhu Gao, 2015). Moreover, the system of indicators must be deployed centrally by the national maritime dynamic supervision system. Finally, the final acceptance and post evaluation of coastal reclamation projects should be improved and enhanced for tracking and monitoring of the marine ecological impact of large-scale coastal reclamation activities and for identifying the need for ecological restoration projects.

10.2.2 *On the Basis of Marine Functional Zoning, a System of Restrictions on Sea-Area Spatial Uses Should Be Strictly Implemented*

The marine functional zoning system is one of the three pillars of sea-area management established by the Law of the People's Republic of China on the Administration of the Use of Sea Areas. The system is the main basis for maintaining the order of sea-area spatial development. Within the primary marine functional zones, industrial and urban construction zones are explicitly established for industrial and urban construction. Large-scale industrial and urban construction projects are allowed in the zones. Nevertheless, no industrial and urban construction projects are permitted in other zone categories. Moreover, the construction projects are subject to control in terms of the total size. The control over their total size is applied by the provincial administrative regions. For coastal reclamation in the industrial and urban construction zones, in addition to the verification of compliance with requirements on overall distribution and management, suitability for coastal reclamation in terms of resources and the environment should also be thoroughly investigated for each zone. The carrying capacity for coastal reclamation can then be estimated within a provincial administrative region on the basis of the suitability, costs, social and economic development, and technical feasibility for construction. The estimated carrying capacity serves as the overall target for controlling the total size of coastal reclamation for the next 50 years in the region. Furthermore, in other zones—such as port and shipping zones, tourism, leisure, and entertainment zones, agricultural and fishery zones, and mining and energy zones—large-scale coastal reclamation in order to build port and pier infrastructure, logistics storage yards, hotels, and restaurants for tourism and entertainment, artificial islands for tourism and entertainment, and minerals and energy storage areas should be strictly controlled. Regulations based on marine functional zoning for restricting sea-area spatial uses should be introduced to refine the management of development activities.

10.2.3 *The Principle of User Pays and a System of Ecological Compensation Should Be Enhanced for the Use of Sea-Area Resources by Coastal Reclamation Projects*

According to the reform initiative of "applying the principle of user pays and a system of ecological compensation for natural resources," proposed by the Third Plenary Session of the 18th National Congress of the Communist Party of China, the existing systems need to be improved further. The existing rate of royalties for sea areas will be adjusted as needed, in line with the value of use rights for coastal reclamation areas, market demand for reclaimed land, national economic development, and affordability, as well as dynamic changes of the land transfer prices of new construction sites. Such an adjustment acts as a tool to fill the gap between royalties and land transfer prices, thereby removing the economic leverage that drives coastal reclamation and increasing the cost of using state-owned sea-area spatial resources. At the same time, this tool is handy for increasing the asset value of the resources and safeguarding the legitimate income of the state owners.

Innovative pollution and damage monitoring and evaluation systems should be introduced for the marine environment, fully taking into consideration the damage caused by coastal reclamation on marine fishery resources, the marine natural landscape, and the service functions of marine ecological systems. A method for evaluating ecological damage and compensation for coastal reclamation activities should also be devised to evaluate the use and damage, how the damage should be compensated for ecologically, and the appropriate rate of compensation appropriately. As the state owner of the sea-area resources, the relevant authorities should collect the ecological compensation charges for the use of or damage to the marine ecological environment. The proceeds will be used for ecological restoration and consolidation of polluted or damaged sea areas. For typical damage to the marine ecological environment, the rate could be doubled to increase the cost incurred for polluting or damaging the marine ecological environment. A marine environment comprehensive consolidation and restoration fund could be established by pooling the compensation charges for pollution and damage, sea-area royalties, compensation charges for sea-area use, and national funds for marine environmental protection (Xiang Lan, 2009b). For treating the pollution and damage, a service provider should be selected through public bidding. Moreover, provisions for implementing and managing the consolidation and restoration projects should be developed to ensure the quality of these projects.

10.2.4 *Adoption of Innovative Mechanisms for Supervising and Evaluating Coastal Reclamation Projects*

The current practice of requiring the owners of coastal reclamation projects to pay for sea-use demonstration, marine environmental impact evaluation, sea-use dynamic monitoring, marine environmental impact tracking and monitoring, and the final acceptance survey should be reformed. Instead, the relevant authorities could collect project management fees from the contractors in the name of ecological compensation charges or supervision fees to cover the cost of the above tasks to improve the objectivity and fairness of the results and the effectiveness of coastal reclamation management.

On the other hand, ocean administrators, supported by a national sea-use dynamic surveillance and monitoring system, could establish a dynamic supervision system covering the whole life cycle of coastal reclamation projects through such means as satellite remote sensing, unmanned aerial vehicle (UAV) monitoring, and field investigations. These techniques could be used for supervising the whole life cycle, managing by category, and controlling the total size. The operation of the sea-use dynamic surveillance and monitoring system at the state, province, city, and county levels makes it possible to capture accurately the developments of coastal reclamation activities in any region nationwide. On the basis of the real-time information, ocean administrators at various levels could develop or adjust their management policies for coastal reclamation as needed. Regular dynamic monitoring at the state level through the monitoring system could also identify noncompliance and illegal activities, which can be corrected in time with the support of enforcement departments to maintain the order of development.

10.2.5 *Improving the Regulations and Policies for Coastal Reclamation Management and Applying Harsher Penalties for Noncompliance and Illegal Activities*

In view of the characteristics of coastal reclamation management and by incorporating relevant laws and regulations, the relevant authorities could issue the Regulations on Coastal Reclamation Management to build a better management framework for managing coastal reclamation activities. The Law of the People's Republic of China on the Administration of the Use of Sea Areas and other relevant laws should be amended in due course to increase the penalties for non-compliance and illegal activities, as well as to enhance the deterrent effect of the law. Furthermore, it should be possible to apply the legal framework for construction land to coastal reclamation activities to ensure that the quota for coastal reclamation and those for new construction sites could be managed simultaneously.

The legal loophole in reclaimed land for agricultural purposes should be closed by making specific regulations on the issue (Jing Li, 2008).

The cooperation between ocean administrators and marine enforcement departments should be enhanced further. In particular, a dedicated task force for sea-area use should be established within the enforcement departments for regular inspection, covering violations such as sea use without approval in advance, exceeding the area approved, altering usage without authorization, submitting multiple applications for a single project, and giving approval without proper authority. The relevant authority should build an effective channel to engage the public in the supervision and management of coastal reclamation activities. Public engagement and supervision in the application, approval, and construction stages of coastal reclamation projects could facilitate the supervision and management of violations.

10.2.6 *Improving Coastal Reclamation Management Techniques through Extensive Research*

The relevant authorities should carry out extensive research on coastal reclamation management techniques to make management decisions that are more informed.

(1) *Leveraging external expertise*: Experts and technicians in the ocean, the economy, planning, law, coastal engineering, and environmental protection could be engaged to establish a marine development expert advisory group, which could assume the role of providing consultation services and systematic technical demonstrations on the relevant marine planning, large-scale coastal reclamation projects, and major sea-area development projects.

(2) *Improving the guidelines for coastal reclamation management*: In accordance with the actual needs of social and economic development in different periods, the relevant authorities could organize a team of experts in planning, engineering, and the ocean to revise or compile the marine functional zoning, improve regional sea-use planning, adjust the rate of royalties, and improve the ecological compensation system for coastal reclamation.

(3) *Carrying out medium- and long-term observation and research on coastal reclamation's impact on resources and environment*: The relevant authorities should guide researchers to apply funding to the national basic research projects, covering continuous and comprehensive tracking, monitoring, evaluating, and studying marine hydrodynamics and erosion/siltation, the service functions of ecological systems, and marine disaster risks for large-scale coastal reclamation projects. The research results could provide technical support for the management of large-scale coastal reclamation projects.

(4) *Greater use of leading technologies to enhance monitoring and management of coastal reclamation projects*: The relevant authorities should examine the possibility of using technologies such as high-precision satellite remote sensing, UAV monitoring, and high-precision offshore positioning on a regular basis in dynamic monitoring and final acceptance of coastal reclamation projects. At the same time, mathematical and physical modeling technologies could be introduced to develop three-dimensional marine models, which could be handy for supervising coastal reclamation projects.

References

Academic Divisions of Chinese Academy of Sciences. Some Scientific Issues and Countermeasures in Coastal Reclamation Projects in China. *Bulletin of the Chinese Academy of Sciences*, 2011, 26 (2): 171–174.

Bao, Xuping, Zhang Zhao, Lv Baoqiang, *et al*. A Brief Discussion on the Design of Dynamic Monitoring Scheme for Sea-Area Use of Coastal Reclamation Projects. *Ocean Development and Management*, 2014, 3: 64–68.

Chen, Shuquan. On Strengthening Environmental Management of Coastal Reclamation Projects in China. *Ocean Development and Management*, 2009, 26 (9): 22–26.

Chengxiang, Xu, Yongqiang Yu. Summary of Beach Reclamation Development in Zhejiang. *Zhejiang Hydrotechnics*, 2003, 1: 8–10.

Chu, Min, Wangchen Liangzi. On Policies for Regulating Coastal Reclamation Projects. *Journal of Ocean University of China (Social Sciences Edition)*, 2011, 22 (2): 81–82.

Department of Sea Area and Island Administration, State Oceanic Administration. Training Materials on Sea-Use Demonstration. Beijing: China Ocean Press, 2012.

Fu, Yuanbin, Zhao Jianhua, Wang Quanming. Discussions on the Sea-Use Dynamic Monitoring System in China. *Journal of Natural Resources*, 2009, 23 (2): 185–193.

Gao, Jinzhu. Preliminary Study on Optimizing Coastal Reclamation Management in China. *Marine Economy*, 2015, 5 (3): 56–62.

Gao, Wenbin, Liu Xiuze, Duan Youyang, *et al*. Effects of Coastal Reclamation Projects on Coastal Fishery Resources in Liaoning Province and the Countermeasures. *Journal of Dalian Fisheries University*, 2009, 24 (S): 18–25.

Gao, Zhiqiang, Liu Xiangyang, Ning Jicai, *et al.* Remote Sensing-Observed Variation of China's Shoreline and Area of Coastal Reclamation in Nearly 30 Years and the Causal Analysis. *Transactions of the Chinese Society of Agricultural Engineering*, 2014, 30 (12): 140–147.

Guan, Daoming, A Dong. Study on National Marine Functional Zoning. Beijing: China Ocean Press, 2013.

He, Qixiang, Zhao Hongwei, *et al.* Integrated Coastal Zone Management in the Netherlands. *Marine Geology Letters*, 2002, 18 (8): 29–33.

Hu, Siliang. On Coastal Reclamation and Its Management System. Qingdao: Ocean University of China, 2011.

Hu, Xiaoying, Zhou Xinghua, Liu Feng, *et al.* Research on Environmental Issues Caused by Coastal Reclamation and Discussions on Management Countermeasures. *Ocean Development and Management*, 2009, 26 (10): 80–86.

Hu, Zong-en, Wang Miao. Setting Evaluation Criteria for the Impact of Coastal Reclamation on Marine Ecological System and Empirical Research. *Marine Environmental Science*, 2016, 35 (3): 357–365.

Huang, Guozhu, Zhu Tan, Cao Ya. Thoughts on Ecological Coastal Reclamation in China and Its Outlook. *Future and Development*, 2013, 5: 18–25.

Huang, Jie, Liang Yahui, Wang Yu. Economic Analysis of Regional Coastal Reclamation in China. *China Economist*, 2016a, 2: 166–167.

Huang, Jie, Suo Anning, Sun Jiawen, *et al.* Driving Mechanism and Demand Forecasting Model of Large-Scale Coastal Reclamation in China. *Journal of Dalian Maritime University (Social Science Edition)*, 2016b, 15 (2): 13–18.

Jia, Kai. System of Indicators for Minimizing Use of Shoreline in Coastal Reclamation. Dalian: Dalian Maritime University, 2012.

Lan, Xiang. Discussions on the Ways for Sustainable Use of Coastal Reclamation Projects. Qingdao: Ocean University of China, 2009a.

Lan, Xiang. Analysis on the Impact of Coastal Reclamation on Marine Industries. *China Water Transport*, 2009b, 9 (5): 88–89.

Li, Jing. Evolution Analysis and Comprehensive Benefit Evaluation of Coastal Reclamation in Hebei Province. Shijiazhuang: Hebei Normal University, 2008.

Li, Jingmei, Liu Tieying. Evaluation of Coastal Reclamation's Ecological Damages to Jiaozhou Bay on the Basis of Habitat Equivalency Analysis. *Acta Ecologica Sinica*, 2012a, 32 (22): 7146–7155.

Li, Jingmei, Sun Xia, Xie Ennian. An Empirical Analysis of the Economic Drivers of Coastal Reclamation. *Chinese Fisheries Economics*, 2012b, 30 (6): 61–68.

Li, Rongjun. Lessons from Coastal Reclamation in the Netherlands. *Ocean Development and Management*, 2006, 23 (3): 31–34.

Lin, Xia, Wang Peng, Jia Kai. GIS-Based Suitability Evaluation of Coastal Reclamation in Liaoning Province. *Ocean Development and Management*, 2015, (5): 27–32.

Liu, Baiqiong, Xu Min, Liu Qing. Comprehensive Evaluation on the Scale of Coastal Reclamation for Port and Port Industries. *Marine Sciences,* 2015, 39 (6): 81–87.

Liu, Baiqiong, Xu Min, Yu Liangliang. Research on the Control Line of Yaosha Coastal Reclamation in Shoal in Northern Jiangsu. *Resources and Environment in the Yangtze Basin,* 2014, 23 (10): 1391–1397.

Liu, Dahai, Feng Aiping, Liu Yang. Discussions on Comprehensive Profit and Loss Evaluation System of Coastal Reclamation. *Coastal Engineering,* 2006, 25 (2): 93–99.

Liu, Hongbin, Sun Li. Game Analysis and Protection Countermeasures for Coastal Reclamation Behaviors in Jiaozhou Bay. *Ocean Development and Management,* 2008, 25 (6): 28–32.

Liu, Shuang, Zhang Jimin, Tang Wei. Brief Discussions on the Urgency of Introducing Ecological Compensation Mechanisms in Management of Coastal Reclamation Projects in China. *Ocean Development and Management,* 2008, 25 (11): 34–37.

Liu, Shuxi, Sun Shuyan. Preliminary Discussions on Evaluating Carrying Capacity for Coastal Reclamation from the Perspective of Ecological System Functions. *Chinese Fisheries Economics,* 2013, 31 (1): 150–154.

Liu, Su, Zhi Jiangyu. Discussions on the Technical Methods for Acceptance Survey of Completed Coastal Reclamation Projects and Several Issues. *Ocean Development and Management,* 2016, 33 (2): 39–42.

Liu, Wei. Analysis of Driving Mechanisms and Controlling of Reclamation Boom. *Natural Resource Economics of China,* 2008, 21 (1): 29–31.

Liu, Yang, Feng Aiping. Methods for Demand Analysis for the Area of Regional Coastal Reclamation. *Chinese Fisheries Economics,* 2011, 29 (6): 92–97.

Lou, Chengwu, Chang Ailian. Reflections on Reclamation Control Policies in China and Its Improvement Measures. *Guangzhou Environmental Science,* 2010, 25 (4): 1–14.

Miao, Fengmin. Introduction to Sea-Use Management Techniques. Beijing: China Ocean Press, 2004.

Miao, Fengmin. Theories and Methods of Sea-Area Grading and Value Assessment. Beijing: China Ocean Press, 2007.

Pan, Xinchun. Introduction to Sea-Area Management. Beijing: China Ocean Press, 2014.

Peng, Benrong, Hong Huasheng, Chen Weiqi. Evaluation of Ecological Damages Due to Coastal Reclamation: Theories, Methods, and Applications. *Journal of Natural Resources,* 2005, 20 (5): 714–726.

Ren, Yuan, Wang Yongzhi. Reflections on Appropriate Coastal Reclamation Based on Local Conditions—A Case Study of Wenzhou. *Periodical of the Ocean University of China (Social Sciences Edition),* 2008, 2: 89–91.

Soma, Katrine, Arild Vatn. Local Democracy Implications for Coastal Zone Management: A Case Study in Southern Norway. *Land Use Policy*, 2009, 3: 755–762.

Song, Derui, Zhao Jianhua, Zhang Yongrong, *et al.* Multi-mode Integrated Sharing of Marine Dynamic Surveillance and Monitoring Data. *Marine Environmental Science*, 2012, 31 (4): 520–524.

Sun, Li. Comparative Study on Coastal Reclamation Management Practices in China and Other Countries. Qingdao: Ocean University of China, 2009.

Sun, Qinbang, Chen Yanzhen, Chen Zhaolin, *et al.* Discussions on Issues in Acceptance Survey of Completed Coastal Reclamation Projects. *Ocean Development and Management*, 2015, 3: 27–29.

Sun, Shuxian. Discussions on Management Measures for Coastal Reclamation Projects. *Ocean Development and Management*, 2004, 21 (6): 21–23.

Suo, Anning, Wang Peng, Yuan Daowei, *et al.* A Study on Monitoring and Evaluation Methods for Existing Coastal Reclamation Resources Based on High Spatial Resolution Satellite Remote Sensing Images. *Acta Oceanologica Sinica*, 2016, 38 (9): 54–63.

Suo, Anning, Minghui Zhang. Sea Areas Reclamation and Coastline Change Monitoring by Remote Sensing in Coastal Zone of Liaoning in China. *Journal of Coastal Research*, 2015, 73: 725–729.

Suo, Anning, Yu Yonghai, Zhao Jianhua, *et al.* Prediction Methods for Coastal Reclamation Demands. *Ocean Development and Management*, 2012a, (7): 17–21.

Suo, Anning, Zhang Minghui, Yu Yonghai. Retrospective Evaluation of Environmental Impact of Caofeidian Reclamation Project. *Environmental Monitoring in China*, 2012b, 28 (2): 105–111.

Suo, Anning, Zhang Minghui, Yu Yonghai. Discussions on Evaluation Methods for Layout Design of Coastal Reclamation Projects. *Coastal Engineering*, 2012c, 31 (1): 28–35.

Suo, Anning, Zhang Minghui, Yu Yonghai, *et al.* Estimation of Loss in Marine Ecological Service Functions Value Caused by Reclamation, A Case Study in Caofeidian. *Marine Sciences*, 2012d, 36 (3): 108–114.

Tang, Minqiang, Liu Wenyong, Wei. Technical Methods of Acceptance Survey of Completed Coastal Reclamation Projects. *Ocean Technology*, 2009, 28 (2): 80–83.

Wang, Guochang, Huang Xiangsui, Li Tianwei, *et al.* Discussion on Post Evaluation of Industrial Comprehensive Development Zones. *Research of Environmental Sciences*, 1999, 12 (1): 30–34.

Wang, Houjun, Ding Ning, Zhao Jianhua, *et al.* Research on Contents and Methods of Dynamic Monitoring of Sea Use by Coastal Reclamation Projects. *Ocean Development and Management*, 2015, 32 (12): 7–10.

Wang, Qi, Tian Yingying. Evaluation and Optimization of China's Coastal Reclamation Policies under the Background of Blue Bay Consolidation. *Periodical of the Ocean University of China (Social Sciences Edition)*, 2016, 4: 42–48.

Wang, Shuguang, Wang Zhiyong, Bao Xianwen. Research on Post Evaluation System for Sea Use in China. *Journal of Oceanography in Taiwan Strait*, 2008, 27 (2): 262–266.

Wang, Yan, Wang Peng, Suo Anning. Implications of Land Resource Reserve System for Marine Resource Management. *Ocean Development and Management*, 2014, 31 (7): 25–29.

Wang, Zhiyong, Wang Shuguang, Bao Xianwen. Preliminary Research on Post Evaluation for Sea Use. *Ocean Development and Management*, 2008, 1: 60–66.

Wen, Guoyi, Yang Jianqiang, Suo Anning. A Study on Technology and Its Application of Coastal Reclamation Layout Optimization for Intensive Sea Use Region. Beijing: China Ocean Press, 2015.

Yao, Li. A Study on Some Issues in Coastal Reclamation Management. Tianjin: Tianjin University, 2007, 11–14.

Yu, Qingsong, Qi Lianming. Theoretical Research on Sea-Area Evaluation. Beijing: China Ocean Press, 2006.

Yu, Yonghai, Suo Anning. Research on Evaluation Methods for Coastal Reclamation. Beijing: China Ocean Press, 2013a.

Yu, Yonghai, Suo Anning. Methods and Practices of Suitability Evaluation for Coastal Reclamation. Beijing: China Ocean Press, 2013b.

Yue, Qi, Xu Wei, Hu Heng, *et al*. Development History and Characteristics of Coastal Reclamation in the World. *Ocean Development and Management*, 2015, 6: 1–5.

Zhang, Minghui, Chen Changping, Suo Anning. Estimation Method for Spatial Capacity of Sea Areas Reclamation. *Applied Mechanics and Materials*, 2013, 260–261: 1026–1029.

Zhu, Ling, Liu Baiqiao. Study on Methods for Evaluating Comprehensive Benefits of Coastal Reclamation Projects. *Ocean Development and Management*, 2009, 26 (2): 113–116.

Index

Printed in the United States
by Baker & Taylor Publisher Services